Have fun in the kitchen!

MK

KITCHEN RITUAL

RECIPES *to* INSPIRE
the ART *and* PRACTICE
of MINDFUL COOKING

. . . .

Meredith Klein

All text and recipes copyright ©2017 by Meredith Klein

All rights reserved.

No part of this book may be reproduced, stored in a retrieval system, or transmitted in any form or by any means without the prior written consent of the author.

ISBN 978-0-692-95701-1

Design by Amy Saidens
Interior photography by Tessa Duff & Sammy Miller
Cover photography by Carrie Lederer & Matt Hollingsworth
Interior illustrations by Olesya Karakotsya©123RF.com, blue67©123RF.com
& Amy Saidens

Printed in the USA

"When you are cooking, you're not just working on food. You're working on yourself. You're working on other people."
— SHUNRYU SUZUKI ROSHI

"A recipe has no soul. You, as the cook, must bring soul to the recipe."
— THOMAS KELLER

CONTENTS

INTRODUCTION	6
BREAKFAST	18
APPETIZERS & SNACKS	36
SOUPS	52
MAINS	72
GRAINS	96
LEGUMES	108
SALADS	120
VEGGIES SIDES	134
DESSERT	160
TEA & SMOOTHIES	176
DRESSINGS & SAUCES	188
PANTRY STAPLES	204
GRATITUDE & ACKNOWLEDGEMENTS	218
INDEX	220

INTRODUCTION

RITUAL

When the title of this book first came to me, several people I shared it with initially discouraged me from using it, worried it would connote an overly religious tone that might put some people off. But for me, when I consider this definition of ritual: *"a series of activities performed in a particular place, and performed according to set sequence,"* I think it perfectly describes what happens in kitchens worldwide—in homes, five-star restaurants, even roadside snack shacks. The simple act of cooking is itself a ritual, one that I find incredibly sacred. It is the ritual of sustenance, the fount from which our life force energy flows.

Each of us shapes the ritual in our own way, drawing influence from family members, friends, and (in this modern age) food bloggers and celebrity TV chefs. We decide which stores and markets we will source our food from and perhaps have a ritualized path by which we circumambulate these locales. Some of us gather and prep every last ingredient before a flame is initiated while others throw things together in a hurried and haphazard way. For some, a meal is always the byproduct of a recipe followed to a tee, and for others of us, a meal just comes together by way of our imaginations.

As someone who has traveled extensively, I notice that no matter how different the kitchens I've visited across the globe may look, there is a core, overarching ritual that transpires within them. Ingredients are procured, various preparations take place (some in a relatively short time, like washing and chopping vegetables; others in days or months, as in the case of pickles and ferments), foods are cooked or arranged, then served and enjoyed.

When we cook using whole food ingredients, especially local and organic produce, we are inextricably connected to the rhythmic rituals of the earth itself. We savor ingredients when they are in season and notice when they disappear from the stalls of our farmers market, only to be replaced by something else.

I hesitate to label this book as an Ayurvedic cookbook or a vegan cookbook, even though both of those categorizations certainly apply. My purest intention with this book is simply to inspire people to spend more time in their kitchens, whether it is to make these recipes or create anything else that inspires them.

We live in a time where despite all of our many newfangled ways of staying connected, I find that people often feel disconnected—from other people, from nature and from who they truly are. Cooking is one of the simplest and most potent ways I've found to remedy this pervasive sense of disconnection, so this book is my contribution to inspiring a more connected planet. I hope you'll use these recipes to feed both yourself and others.

I would love to hear (and see!) how this book inspires you. Please stay connected and feel free to share your experiences in written, photographic and video form:
Facebook: www.facebook.com/bepranaful/
Instagram: @pranaful
Twitter: @pranaful
e-mail: mer@pranaful.com

INTRODUCTION

IS THIS A VEGAN COOKBOOK?

Well, yes . . . and no. Nearly all my recipes are vegan/plant-based with a few exceptions. Where non-vegan ingredients are used, I always provide a vegan substitution, so vegan cooks will find this to be a very friendly book.

While I was once a self-described "hardcore militant vegan," those days are long gone, and I'm much happier for it. Part of my personal journey has been to let go of all the labels attached to my food. I mean this in the sense of ditching processed and packaged foods that come with physical labels as well as the labels that are so commonly used to describe myriad dietary preferences that our ancestors would certainly not recognize.

The one label I do sometimes attach to myself is "love-atarian." I'd much prefer to eat a lovingly prepared feast made by someone I know than stick to any one piece of dietary dogma. After years of restricting myself and turning down so much food from friends, loved ones and numerous hosts abroad, it feels so much better to me to at least have a taste of whatever is offered.

The recipes in this book represent my personal preferences and are reflective of what I choose to prepare for myself on a daily basis. Plant-based foods leave me feeling light and energized in my body, and help me as an ordained and practicing Buddhist to feel I am doing some part to reduce suffering in the world.

I fully respect each person's dietary preferences and choices and recognize that labels do work for some people. Whoever you are and whatever your labels (or lack thereof), I hope you will find the recipes in this book delicious and that they will inspire you to spend more time nourishing yourself with food you have created.

ANCIENT WISDOM FOR A MODERN KITCHEN

Much of my training outside of the kitchen has been in Ayurveda, a 5,000-year-old healing science that is indigenous to India. A key tenet of Ayurveda is the notion that food is medicine, so as you prepare these recipes, know that I have very intentionally paired certain foods, chosen particular spices, and eschewed some practices of Western cooking (like putting black pepper into everything) for a reason. The great news is that I have done all the work for you, and you do not need to know a single thing about Ayurveda to benefit from this ancient wisdom.

SACRED SPACE IN THE KITCHEN

I perhaps first became aware of the way a chef's energy affects a meal when I worked as the "take-out girl" at a Chinese restaurant while in high school in Texas. There were two chefs—the owner, John, a kind man in his late 40s from Taiwan, and a guy named Tom. Both were frequently in the kitchen on the weekend evenings when I tended to work. It didn't take long before I could tell after just one or two bites which chef had made the fried rice or sautéed string beans that I would snack on during my breaks from scooping fragrant white rice into small white boxes and packing up bags with paper cartons and fortune cookies.

Both John and Tom were excellent cooks, but I could pick up on subtle differences in the food they prepared. I remember one day when Tom was in a particularly foul mood, banging pots around and scowling at everyone in the kitchen. That day, I remember thinking the food was off as I ate my mid-shift snack. I think it is the only time I can remember one of our customers sending a dish back. He could taste it too. At the time, I didn't have the understanding or vocabulary to describe what I perceived as energy, but from where I stand today, I know that was the invisible ingredient my sensitive palate was detecting.

In Ayurveda (and other traditions as well), it's said that you must digest everything—not just the physical meal, but all experiences, all energy you take on. If you're eating food prepared with love and intention, it will pass through you differently than food prepared by someone consumed with rage and anxiety. I've read interviews with macrobiotic chefs who recognize the importance of the moods of everyone handing the food and will ask their sous chefs to leave their shift early if they can sense they are not in a good headspace.

Similarly, Café Gratitude, a chain of vegan restaurants that started in the San Francisco Bay area, would require its kitchen staff as well as all other employees to "clear" their energy when arriving for work, consciously taking a moment to sit down with a manager and release whatever "stuff" they'd arrived with that day. I believe this is a good practice for all chefs to engage in. Even just taking three deep, conscious breaths before beginning your meal prep can be helpful. As you exhale, try releasing any worries, plans, or other thoughts that have been occupying your mind. Allow yourself to fully arrive in the kitchen and be present to the task at hand.

Another thing I like to do to clear the energy of the kitchen before I begin cooking is to light a candle. I always keep a candle in the kitchen. You may choose to keep one as part of a kitchen altar, which you'll commonly find in the kitchens of observant Buddhist and Hindu practitioners. This is a small sacred space to remind you of the important, life-sustaining work that takes place there. You might keep flowers, rocks or crystals, items with inspirational messages or other tokens of a religious or non – religious nature on your kitchen altar. If counter space is at a premium, try using a windowsill, the top of the refrigerator, or some other unused space for your altar, or you can install a small shelf to house it.

INTRODUCTION

To treat the kitchen as a sacred space means keeping it clean. If the kitchen is not tidy when you arrive to cook, the inclination can be just to start, because you're going to get things dirty soon anyhow. If this is your habit, I would encourage you to take a couple minutes to straighten up before you begin, allowing yourself to start fresh, like an artist with a clean, fresh canvas.

As part of your preparation and clearing process, you should put away all dishes sitting in the dishrack or in the dishwasher if they're clean. This is probably my least favorite task. For many years when I lived on my own, I was a compulsive piler when it came to the dishrack, challenging myself to beat my personal best of how much stuff I could pile on the already-dry dishes as a means of avoiding the process of emptying the rack. I can thank my husband, Francis, for retraining me in this area, and I must say nothing feels better at the end of a meal than going to wash dishes and having a spacious, empty rack in which to place them.

Once your mind is clear and the kitchen is clean, you're ready to begin. As you move through your culinary process, take the time to wash dishes rather than letting them pile up, and tidy counters as you go. As you regularly tend to the space, be sure to intermittently create space within yourself. Take frequent pauses as you cook to remember your breath and body. Notice if you've become so fixated on the end product that you forget to enjoy yourself in the process. Remember that the energy you put out will be flavoring the meal, so take every precaution you can to make your own "special sauce" a good one.

SETTING UP THE MINDFUL KITCHEN

In any sphere of life, the right tools make every task easier. Some people have cobbled together kitchens that are barely functional. They will improvise a plate for a pot lid, and find myriad uses for a single fork. Others have stocked their kitchens with more items than they could ever possibly use, filling drawers, cabinets and boxes in garages.

A well-stocked kitchen has exactly what the cook needs—no more, no less. Every item has a purpose, if not many. Materials are in good working order and replaced once they are broken or otherwise ineffective. Each item has a dedicated home where it can be found day after day; no time is wasted searching for gadgets or tracking down the corresponding lid for a pot.

The following is my list of kitchen essentials. There likely are a few additional things in your kitchen right now that you simply could not live without. You don't need to hold yourself to this list, but it does provide a baseline for establishing a very functional home kitchen space.

Quality Cookware: When choosing cookware, quality certainly trumps quantity. It is not necessary to purchase a 15 – or 20-piece set, although sometimes purchasing a smaller set can be a cost-effective way to stock your kitchen. Personally, I have bought each piece of my cookware individually to fulfill a very specific need. I consider these essential pieces: a large soup pot, small and medium saucepans, and at least two skillets of varying sizes. Avoid toxic non-stick products and choose stainless steel, cast iron, or enameled cast iron cookware whenever possible.

Kitchen Timer: Even if your stove has a timer, a small kitchen timer that you can take with you to another room of your home (or outdoors) is very handy to have for dishes that take some time to cook or bake. There is nothing more disappointing than failing to hear a timer and burning a batch of goodies in the oven. Likewise, we sometimes fail to use a timer, thinking instead we will remember when to turn a flame off, and inevitably we get wrapped up in something else and fail to remember. Or we may be unable to fully dedicate our attention to our next task because we are repeatedly checking the clock. Use a timer so you can be fully present with your next task in the kitchen. I like using an old-school dial timer that rings a nice bell when time is up. The bell can be used both as a reminder that something is done and as a bell of mindfulness to reconnect you to your breathing and your body. Your phone can certainly be used, but I encourage you to be mindful of the distractions it may introduce into your workspace.

Large Cutting Board: Unless you're lucky enough to have a built-in butcher-block countertop, I recommend finding the biggest board that can comfortably fit on your favorite prep space in your kitchen. Avoid plastic or glass, and choose a wood surface instead. Wood is less likely to harbor bacteria and less damaging to your knives. You can maximize the life of your wood boards by rubbing them with a thin coating of food-grade mineral oil every month or two. If your countertop is uneven (e.g., tiled) or slippery, consider buying a silicon mat to place under your board for stability.

INTRODUCTION

Good Knives: As with cookware, a large set is not necessarily better. Most people I know own a large knife block with 10–20 knives but rarely use all of them. If you care properly for your knives, a large French chef's knife or Santoku (Japanese-style chef's knife) and a smaller paring knife will cover all cutting jobs in the kitchen required in this book. If you prepare meat, make or buy bread, or cut cakes often, it makes sense to have quality knives for those specific tasks as well. It is essential to have a sharpening steel for honing your knives (for more on this, see p. 15), and to have your knives professionally sharpened (about once a year is sufficient for most home chefs).

Mason Jars: I don't think anyone can have too many of these. You can sprout seeds, house items purchased in bulk bins, store leftovers and shake up a dressing, to name just a few of their uses. Mason jars are a chef's best friend. I usually buy mine by the case in all different sizes. Of course, any jar will do the trick, but I love the aesthetic look of Mason jars and appreciate being able to easily replace the lids if they get worn out or rusted.

Measuring Cups or Spoons: Make sure to have a full set of both. If pieces have disappeared over the years, it's worth the investment to buy a new full set. Most importantly, try to find pieces that do not have markings that will rub off with use and washing. Metal spoons and dry measuring cups that have the quantities etched into each piece are my preference, along with a glass measuring cup for liquids.

Wooden Spoons: I visit more kitchens without wooden spoons than you might imagine. These are essential for stirring and sautéing, and won't scratch sensitive cookware surfaces (e.g., enamel) like metal utensils do, and are far more elegant (and safe) than plastic. I prefer buying spoons with a solid handle because I've found thin handles can snap under pressure when moving through a thick dough or hearty stew.

Whisk: A great whisk is essential. If you feel kind of "meh" about your whisk, or if it's become wonky and misshapen after many years of use, get a new one that feels amazing in your hand. You'll thank yourself later.

Immersion Blender: This tool is perhaps my favorite and is essential for making pureed soups, stews and other delights. If you usually use your blender for such feats, your life will be revolutionized once you get your hands on one of these nifty things, also sometimes called stick blenders. Gone will be the days of transferring hot liquids to the blender (and risking them blowing up in your face!), and you'll have fewer dishes to wash. Win-win.

Food Processor: I grew up in the home of a food processor maven. My mom instilled a deep respect for the Cuisinart in me from an early age. I don't use it as much as she did, but it's vital for many of my favorite things: pestos, raw pie crusts and shredding large amounts of veggies in no time at all. A mini-food processor is great for smaller jobs. You can sometimes find immersion blenders that come with a mini-food processor attachment and check two items off this list at once.

INTRODUCTION

Good Blender: I went to the effort to include "good" here because so many people eke by with a blender they got at the drugstore, only to have it break a year or two down the line, and then replace it with another so-so blender. It can be easy to balk at the cost of a commercial-grade blender, but trust me when I say it is so worth it. They're built to last a lifetime, and the motor is super powerful. Check craigslist, eBay or yard sales for good deals on a used one.

Spice Grinder: You'll unlock a whole new world of flavor when you start grinding your own spices. A spice mill is a great investment, but a cheaper option is to use a coffee grinder. If you go this route, keep a separate grinder for coffee beans unless you enjoy cumin-flavored coffee!

Citrus Juicer: There are many options here. I personally love my electric citrus juicer, but many people don't like to clean them. A handheld juicer is preferred by some, but be sure to get a metal variety—the plastic ones almost always crack over time. A vintage orange juicer with a handle you pull down to crush whatever citrus goodness you've placed between its metal plates is also an effective option. Bottom line: any tool is better than squeezing with your hands alone.

Nut Milk Bag: You can do so many things with this simple little mesh bag. In addition to being able to make your own fresh almond or hazelnut milk, you can also use this handy bag to strain just about anything, including quinoa or other grains you've just washed.

Vegetable Peeler: You probably already own one, but if you don't own a "Y-style" peeler, chances are you're struggling more than you need to. This is the variety chefs prefer and for good reason. You can find good ones for around $5. They'll peel both hard things (like butternut squash and potatoes) and softer items (like mangoes) with ease.

Spoon Rest: Avoid unnecessary splatters and stains on your stovetop by having a dedicated spoon rest. I like to use a small colorful sushi plate.

Water Boiler: When a recipe calls for hot water, I like the instant access a water boiler gives me while also freeing up burner space on the stove. It's also a wonder to have around for making tea or coffee in no time.

Silicone Spatula: Reduce food waste by using one of these to scrape down those elusive last bits of food in bowls, pots, the food processor and the blender. A mini - spatula is great for scraping out small jars, bowls, and so on.

Dough Scraper/Bench Scraper: If you don't know what this handy-dandy tool is, Google it. Then, say hello to your new best friend. Use this tool instead of your knife blade to transfer chopped ingredients to pots or mixing bowls, saving both time and mess.

INTRODUCTION

Inspiring Dishware: In addition to these items for cooking, I cannot stress enough the importance of having dishware that makes you happy. If you're simply using hand-me-downs or boring pieces you picked up at IKEA, consider slowly building a set of fun and inspiring dishware that makes you smile. It may or may not match; it may consist of pieces that are round, square, oval or irregular; it may be patterned or a singular color. Similarly, find napkins, flatware and serving pieces that inspire you. Whatever you decide, let it be reflective of your personality, and each meal will be instantly enhanced.

Making the Most of Any Space: Depending on the size of your kitchen, and the availability (or lack thereof) of a large pantry, it can be challenging to figure out where to store everything in your kitchen. If counter space is limited, try to reserve it for only items that you'll use daily or at least regularly. Try to house less-used items in cabinets, or consider adding shelves as space permits to keep counters uncluttered.

A hanging pot rack can be ideal for kitchens with limited cabinet space. You can also find (or make your own) risers to go within cabinets, adding extra layers of storage space. Hooks on the bottom of shelves or cabinets, magnetized hangers off the side of the refrigerator, and countless other solutions exist for making the most of even the smallest space. You don't need a huge kitchen to make cooking easy; you simply need a well-organized space.

Keep Only Items Related To Food Preparation In Your Kitchen: That may sound simple, but for many people, the kitchen serves as a storeroom for so many other things or as a secondary home office. If an item in your kitchen doesn't directly assist you in preparing food, find it another home.

THE BEST PIECE OF FREE KITCHEN EQUIPMENT

Many people don't make use of the best kitchen tool you cannot buy: your hands. When tossing a large salad, massaging kale, mixing dough, or doing countless other tasks, your hands are often the most efficient tool. Many people in our germophobic culture seem wary of touching food (or having others touch theirs), but with clean hands, you are good to go. In addition to being efficient, using your hands engages your sense of touch and allows you to connect with your food in a deeper way.

KNIFE SKILLS 101

Knowing how to handle and care for a knife is perhaps the single most important thing you can learn to increase both efficiency and safety in your personal kitchen rituals. I recommend taking a knife skills class in your area if available—the return on your investment will be exponential. For now, here are some essential tips to keep in mind.

Expensive is Not Always Better: One of the best knives I own is a $5 knife from IKEA. Similarly, many professional chefs swear by cheap knives they pick up at a local Asian market. Bottom line: spending a lot of money on a great knife is completely optional.

Look for the Goldilocks Moment: When you shop for a knife, try out many and look for one that just feels right in your hand. Not every knife feels good to everyone. Find the one that feels like it was custom made for your hand.

Sharpening vs. Honing: Many people own a sharpening steel—a long tool people like to call a knife sharpener—but that name is deceptive; this tool hones your knife but doesn't actually sharpen it. Honing is the process by which the very edge of the knife gets groomed and fine-tuned into its proper angle. You should hone your knife at least once a week, if not every time you cook. Sharpening is handled by a professional, and most home chefs will be fine with one sharpening session per year. If you haven't had your knives professionally sharpened in over a year, please do that right away. You'll thank me later.

Hold Your Knife Properly: Your thumb and forefinger should both grip the sides of the blade. Your forefinger never goes on top of the knife—doing so reduces stability and control.

Scraping: Resist the urge to use the sharp side of your knife for scraping your cutting board (see p. 13 and consider getting a bench scraper). To gather items like herbs while chopping, use the top (i.e., the dull edge) of the blade.

Make a Claw: Don't place your fingertips in the line of duty. Your non-dominant hand should form the shape of a claw with your fingertips tucked in for protection.

Cleaning and Care: Never leave dirty knives in a sink full of dishes. This is a great way to end up in the ER. Never put your knives in the dishwasher. Always wash knives by hand and either carefully dry them immediately or place them on a dry surface where excess water won't collect.

This Most Important Rule of Knife Skills: Never attempt to catch a falling knife. Our instinct is to catch falling items, so I recommend repeating this mantra to yourself each time you handle a knife until it becomes engrained in your mind. If you do drop a knife, immediately back away to protect your legs and feet as well.

USEFUL INFORMATION

Unless otherwise specified, use medium or average-size produce for the best results in all recipes.

Use this key to interpret the symbols accompanying each recipe:

 Vegan

 Gluten-Free

 Vegan Option Suggested

 Gluten-Free Option Suggested

The preparation and cooking times are all estimates and will vary depending on the speed at which you work in the kitchen, the cookware that you use, and so on. For recipes with longer cooking times, you can often prep other recipes or wash dishes.

Stove heats vary, so treat heat cues as recommendations. If you are using an electric stove or a smaller burner, you may need to adjust the heat up.

I've tried as much as possible to use accessible ingredients that you can easily find when in season. I do use a robust variety of spices and realize they may not be accessible locally for all readers of this book. To order spices online, I recommend Spice Station: http://spicestationsilverlake.com

Almost every recipe in this book can be adjusted to your preferences. Don't be afraid to omit ingredients or add in something that calls to you. Treat these as rough blueprints rather than rigid design specs.

Most importantly, as one of my culinary heroes, Samin Nosrat, would say:
DON'T FORGET TO HAVE FUN!

BREAKFAST

SAVORY MILLET CEREAL

SPICED MAPLE PECAN GRANOLA

STEEL-CUT OATS WITH PERSIMMON, DATES & TOASTED PUMPKIN SEEDS

CURRIED STEEL-CUT OATS

BANANA BREAD

BANANA BUCKWHEAT PANCAKES

QUINOA PORRIDGE

TOFU GARDEN SCRAMBLE

CHIA SEED PUDDING BREAKFAST BOWLS

COCONUT PECAN SCONES

BREAKFAST

SERVES
4

PREP TIME
5 minutes

COOK TIME
45-55 minutes

TOTAL TIME
50-55 minutes

SAVORY MILLET CEREAL

This warm cereal is a favorite on the retreats I cater, and a nice alternative to sweet oatmeal dishes. This recipe is inspired by the breakfast cereal served at Siddha Yoga meditation centers worldwide.

½ cup millet

1 Tablespoon ghee or coconut oil

1 teaspoon salt

4 cups water

1 teaspoon cumin seeds

¼ teaspoon fenugreek seeds

⅓ cup unsweetened coconut flakes

Half of a yellow or white onion, diced

1 serrano chile, halved lengthwise, seeds removed *

Place millet, ghee/oil, salt and water in a pot and bring to a boil over high heat. Add cumin, fenugreek, coconut, onion and chile (if using), cover the pot, and lower heat to an active simmer. Cook cereal for 45-55 minutes, stirring occasionally, until millet and coconut are very soft and a porridge consistency is achieved.

Serve immediately, or refrigerate and reheat individual portions. When reheating, you may need to add a tablespoon or two of water, as the millet will often absorb all excess liquid as it sits.

*Optional; other mild chile varieties are fine but don't use jalapenos

BREAKFAST

SERVES
6–8

PREP TIME
5 minutes

COOK TIME
45 minutes

TOTAL TIME
50 minutes

SPICED MAPLE PECAN GRANOLA

Once you realize how easy it is to make your own granola, I promise you won't want to eat it from a box again! You'll save money and your kitchen will smell delightful. I encourage you to try swapping out different seeds, nuts and fruits to find the combinations you most enjoy.

3½ cups rolled oats (certified gluten-free if necessary)

¾ cup sunflower seeds

2 Tablespoons chia seeds

2 Tablespoons black sesame seeds

½ cup pecans or other nuts, roughly chopped

2 teaspoons ground ginger

1 teaspoon ground cardamom

Pinch of salt

⅔ cup maple syrup

⅓ cup grapeseed, sunflower or other neutral oil

1 teaspoon maple extract (optional)

⅓ cup dried mulberries

½ cup raisins

Pre-heat oven to 300 degrees. Line 2 standard-sized baking sheets with parchment paper.

In a large bowl, stir together oats, seeds, nuts, spices and salt until well combined. In a small bowl, whisk together maple syrup, oil and maple extract (if using). Pour over the dry ingredients, and stir well to coat.

Spread half of the granola on each baking sheet in a single even layer. Bake for 40 mintes, stirring the granola gently at the 20-minute mark. After 40 minutes, gently stir in half of the mulberries and raisins to each tray and bake for 5 minutes more. Remove trays from the oven and let the granola cool completely before transferring it to a large glass jar or other airtight container for storage. (Note that when granola is finished cooking, it may still be slightly sticky. It will harden as it cools.)

BREAKFAST

SERVES
6

PREP TIME
5 minutes

COOK TIME
45 minutes

TOTAL TIME
50 minutes

STEEL-CUT OATS WITH PERSIMMON, DATES & TOASTED PUMPKIN SEEDS

This is the perfect warm breakfast for cool fall mornings when persimmons are in season. When they are out of season, you can substitute other fresh fruit in their place or use dried fruit.

1 cup steel-cut oats (certified gluten-free if necessary)

4 cups water

½ cup raw pumpkin seeds

1 Tablespoon maple syrup (optional)

1 large Fuyu persimmon, pitted and chopped

8 dates, chopped

Place oats and water in a medium saucepan. Bring to a boil over high heat, then reduce heat to low and cover pot. Cook for 40 minutes stirring occasionally.

While oats cook, heat a small skillet over medium-high flame. When hot, add pumpkin seeds, and cook for 3-4 minutes until seeds are lightly browned and becoming fragrant. Remove from heat to cool.

Once oats are done cooking, stir in toasted pumpkin seeds and all remaining ingredients and cook uncovered for an additional 3-5 minutes. Serve immediately.

BREAKFAST

SERVES
4

PREP TIME
5 minutes

COOK TIME
45 minutes

TOTAL TIME
50 minutes

CURRIED STEEL-CUT OATS

This is a delicious warm savory cereal to get your digestive fire (known as *agni* in Ayurveda) powered up for the day ahead. Make a batch ahead of time and reheat individual portions for a quick breakfast.

1 cup steel-cut oats (certified gluten-free if necessary)

4 cups water

2 teaspoons ghee (substitute coconut oil for vegan option)

1 medium red onion, thinly sliced into half-moons

1 Tablespoon mild curry powder

¼ teaspoon salt

Place oats and water in a medium saucepan and bring to a boil over a high flame. Reduce heat to a very gentle simmer, cover pot and let oats cook for 35 minutes, stirring occasionally.

While oats cook, heat ghee or oil in a medium-sized skillet over a medium flame, then add onion. Cook for 5 minutes or until onion begins to soften and turn translucent, then reduce heat to low and continue cooking for 20–25 minutes over low heat, allowing onion to gently caramelize. Stir occasionally to prevent sticking and burning.

After oats have cooked for 35 minutes, uncover and stir in curry powder, salt and caramelized onions. Allow oats to cook an additional 10–15 minutes uncovered, adding a bit more water if a thinner consistency is desired. Before serving, add any additional curry powder or salt to taste.

BREAKFAST

MAKES
2 loaves

PREP TIME
10 minutes

COOK TIME
45–55 minutes

TOTAL TIME
55–65 minutes

BANANA BREAD

This is my healthier take on my mom's banana bread recipe. The recipe makes two loaves, so you can share one with a friend or pop the extra in the freezer. This recipe works splendidly with gluten-free flour mixes.

3 prepared flax eggs (see p. 208)

5 large ripe bananas*

¼ cup unsweetened almond milk (or milk of your choice)

1 Tablespoon apple cider vinegar

1½ teaspoons baking soda

1½ cups coconut sugar (or other dry sweetener)

¾ cup sunflower oil (or other neutral oil)

1 teaspoon vanilla extract

2¼ cups all-purpose flour (regular or gluten-free)

½ teaspoon salt

1 cup chopped walnuts (optional)

Preheat oven to 350 degrees. Lightly oil two standard-size loaf pans.

In a small bowl, mash bananas well with a fork.

In a large mixing bowl, mix together vinegar and almond milk. Let this sit a couple minutes, then add baking soda (mixture will foam). Add in coconut sugar, oil, vanilla and the flax eggs, and stir well. Add the bananas and mix again, then add flour and salt and combine until everything is well incorporated. Fold in nuts gently, if using.

Pour half the batter into each of the two prepared pans. Bake for 45-55 minutes, until tops are firm and an inserted toothpick comes out with relatively few crumbs attached. Cool for 20 minutes before removing from pans, and let bread finish cooling on wire racks. Finished bread should be stored in sealed containers, on the countertop for up to 48 hours and in the refrigerator thereafter.

I save peeled overripe bananas in a container in my freezer and defrost them for this recipe.

BREAKFAST

BANANA BUCKWHEAT PANCAKES

MAKES
10–12 pancakes

PREP TIME
10 minutes

COOK TIME
15–20 minutes

TOTAL TIME
25–35 minutes

Buckwheat flour gives these pancakes a beautiful dark color and delicious nutty flavor. Buckwheat is a nutrient-dense superfood, making these pancakes an incredibly smart way to start your day.

2 prepared flax eggs (see p. 208)

1 large ripe banana, mashed well with a fork

1 Tablespoon coconut oil, melted and slightly cooled, plus extra for cooking

¾ cup + 1 Tablespoon almond milk (or milk of your choice)

2 teaspoons maple syrup

1 cup buckwheat flour

1 teaspoon baking powder

½ teaspoon cinnamon

¼ teaspoon salt

For serving: Maple syrup and/or fresh fruit

Preheat oven to 200 degrees.

In a medium mixing bowl, whisk together flax eggs, banana, coconut oil, almond milk and maple syrup. Mix together dry ingredients in a small bowl, then whisk into the wet ingredients until a smooth batter is achieved.

In a large skillet, melt about 2 tablespoons coconut oil over medium heat. Once skillet is hot (you can test the heat of the skillet by flicking a drop of water onto the skillet—it will sizzle a bit if it's hot), spoon about ¼ to ⅓ cup of batter into the skillet. When small bubbles begin to percolate up to the surface near the middle of the pancake, you know it's time to flip it over using a spatula. Cook the second side about 2 minutes, or until just golden brown.

Transfer finished pancakes to an ovenproof plate, and keep them in the preheated oven while you repeat the process above for the remaining batter. Reduce the flame at any point if pancakes are getting too dark, and add more oil to the skillet if it becomes dry. Serve pancakes immediately with syrup and/or fruit. Leftovers can easily be reheated in a toaster oven for a quick breakfast.

BREAKFAST

SERVES
4

PREP TIME
10 minutes

TOTAL TIME
10 minutes
+ overnight soak

QUINOA PORRIDGE

This make-ahead breakfast is a great way to utilize leftover quinoa you may have on hand. By letting it sit overnight, the sugars in the fruit gently sweeten the porridge, with no added sugars needed. If you prefer the porridge sweeter, you can drizzle some honey or maple syrup on top when serving.

2 cups (packed) cooked quinoa

2½ cups hemp milk (see page 212 to make your own)

½ cup chopped dried apricots

¼ cup dried cherries

¼ cup walnuts

¼ cup pumpkin seeds

¾ teaspoon ground cinnamon

½ teaspoon vanilla extract

Pinch sea salt

Optional: Honey/maple syrup to drizzle when serving, additional hemp milk

Place all ingredients in a very large jar (or other container with a lid). Seal and shake the jar to combine (or stir together if using a container, then seal). Place in refrigerator overnight.

In the morning, porridge can be eaten cold/at room temperature, or lightly warmed. Add a bit more hemp milk when serving and/or heating, if desired. For a sweeter porridge, drizzle with honey or maple syrup over individual portions.

Feel free to substitute dried fruits and/or nuts and seeds of your choice for what I've suggested. The items I've listed are my favorite things to use, but the possibilities are limitless. You can also garnish the porridge with additional dried or fresh fruits, nuts, seeds, etc.

BREAKFAST

TOFU GARDEN SCRAMBLE

SERVES
4–5

Get a start on your veggie intake for the day with this easy, savory scramble. You can substitute any vegetables/greens you may have around for the ones I suggest here. This scramble makes a great filling for breakfast tacos—simply place in small tortillas of your choice, and serve with fresh salsa or pico de gallo and/or sliced avocado.

PREP TIME
10 minutes

COOK TIME
20 minutes

TOTAL TIME
30 minutes

2 16-ounce packages extra-firm tofu (sprouted if available; not water-packed)

1½ teaspoons chile powder

1 teaspoon ground cumin

3 Tablespoons olive oil, divided

1 small red bell pepper, thinly sliced

8–10 white or crimini mushrooms, sliced

5–6 leaves Swiss chard, chopped into bite-sized pieces

Salt

In a medium mixing bowl, use your fingers to break apart and crumble the tofu. Work until it roughly resembles the texture of cooked ground meat. Add chile powder, cumin and ¾ teaspoon salt. Mix well and set aside.

In a large skillet, heat two tablespoons of oil over medium heat. Add the peppers and sauté 2–3 minutes, until they begin to soften. Add mushrooms and cook until they are soft and glistening. Add the additional tablespoon of oil, then stir in the spiced tofu mixture and reduce heat to medium-low. Cook for 8–10 minutes, until tofu is warmed through, stirring occasionally. Add chard and continue cooking until it is soft, about another 3–4 minutes. Taste and adjust salt or other spices as desired. Serve immediately.

BREAKFAST

SERVES
2

PREP TIME
5 minutes

TOTAL TIME
10 minutes
+ overnight soak

CHIA SEED PUDDING BREAKFAST BOWLS

Chia seed pudding is one of my favorite summer breakfasts. This version uses coconut milk, making it extra cooling for particularly hot days. I'm also a big fan of packing it to go on road trips—I just use a bigger jar so that I can add toppings right in.

¼ cup chia seeds

1 15-ounce can full-fat coconut milk

½ teaspoon maple syrup

⅛ teaspoon vanilla bean powder or ¼ teaspoon vanilla extract

Toppings of your choice: cacao nibs, coconut flakes, fresh berries, sliced banana or mango, granola, seeds, nuts, etc.

Mix all ingredients together in a mason jar or other container with a lid.

Seal jar/container and place in refrigerator overnight to allow chia to plump and set.

To serve, divide chia pudding into individual serving bowls and arrange toppings over it.

· · **CACAO VARATION** · ·

Add 1 tablespoon of raw cacao powder to recipe above and increase maple syrup to one full teaspoon

BREAKFAST

MAKES
9–10 scones

PREP TIME
10 minutes

COOK TIME
45–55 minutes

TOTAL TIME
55–65 minutes

COCONUT PECAN SCONES

These easy scones are a delicious way to start the day, especially when served straight out of the oven. You can substitute different fruit and nut combinations for the coconut and pecans—I've included some ideas at the end of the recipe.

1 cup whole wheat pastry flour

1 cup unbleached all-purpose flour

3 teaspoons baking powder

½ teaspoon salt

1 stick chilled butter (or vegan butter), cut into small cubes

⅔ cup rolled oats

¾ cup almond milk (or milk of your choice)

⅓ cup maple syrup

1 teaspoon maple extract (or substitute vanilla extract)

⅔ cup sliced dried coconut (sometimes labeled "large flakes")

⅓ cup chopped pecans

Preheat oven to 375 degrees. Line a baking sheet with parchment paper (or lightly grease).

Combine the two flours, baking powder and salt in a large bowl. Add the cubes of chilled butter and use a pastry cutter or your fingers to work it into the dry ingredients. You're done when a somewhat grainy mixture is achieved; do not overwork. Gently stir in the oats.

In a small bowl, whisk together the almond (or other) milk, maple syrup and maple extract. Pour this over the wet ingredients, along with the coconut and pecans and use a wooden spoon to stir well until a sticky dough is achieved.

Scoop out about ¼ cup of dough at a time, gently shaping with lightly-oiled hands if you wish, and place each scone on the prepared baking sheet.

Bake until golden brown, about 18-22 minutes (cooking time will vary depending on size of scones and your oven). Let scones cool about 10 minutes, then serve. Scones are best the same day they are made, but will keep for a day or two in a sealed container. Leftovers are best lightly warmed in a toaster or regular oven before serving.

·· OTHER FLAVOR COMBINATIONS TO TRY ··

Dried cranberries and orange zest

· · · · · · · · ·

Chopped dates and walnuts

· · · · · · · · ·

Dried currants and lemon zest

· · · · · · · · ·

Crystallized ginger and dried fig

· · · · · · · · ·

Dried cherries and dark chocolate chips

· · · · · · · · ·

Dried blueberries and chopped almonds

· · · · · · · · ·

Dried apricot and ginger

· · · · · · · · ·

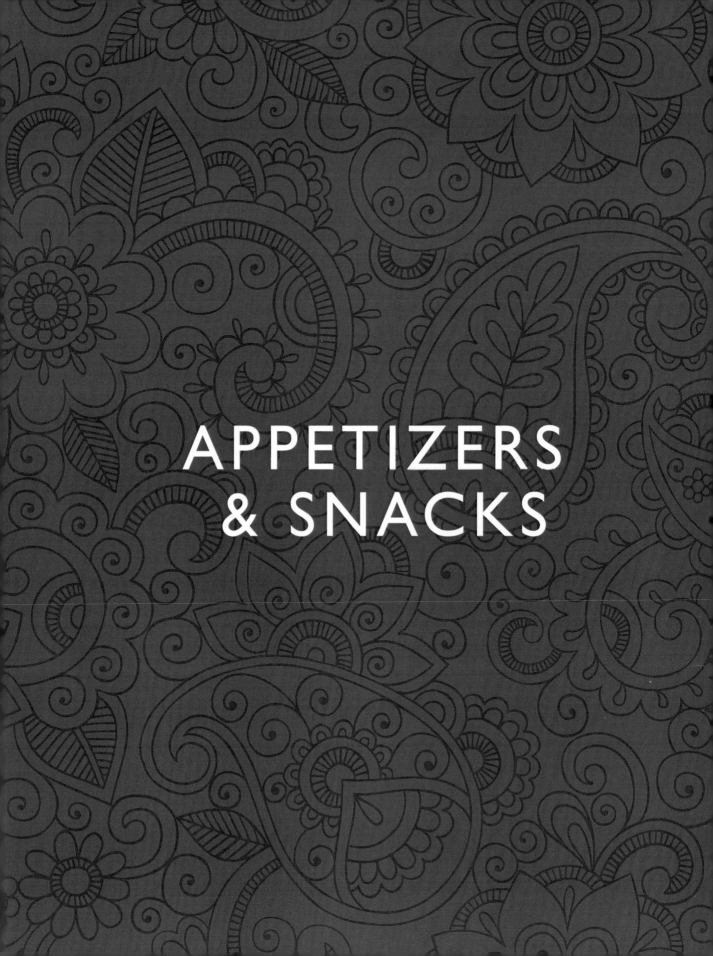

APPETIZERS & SNACKS

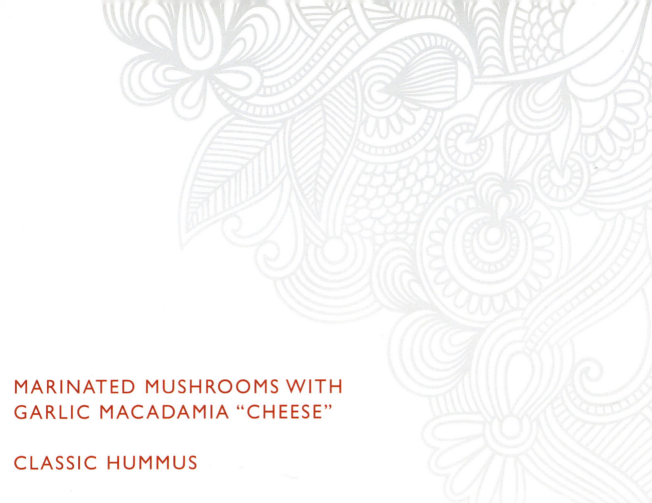

MARINATED MUSHROOMS WITH
GARLIC MACADAMIA "CHEESE"

CLASSIC HUMMUS

ROASTED BUTTERNUT SQUASH HUMMUS

BLACK LENTIL HUMMUS

CURRIED RED LENTIL DIP

ARUGULA & ARTICHOKE DIP

ZESTY KALE CHIPS

GUACAMOLE THREE WAYS

GARAM MASALA POPCORN

APPETIZERS & SNACKS

MAKES
35–40

PREP TIME
15 minutes

TOTAL TIME
15 minutes
+ soaking & resting time

MARINATED MUSHROOMS WITH GARLIC MACADAMIA "CHEESE"

These are one of my go-to party appetizers, and guests always love them. You can use different fillings as well—I will often will make two batches of mushrooms, then stuff half with pesto, and half with the macadamia filling below. Letting the macadamia filling rest overnight allows a true cheesy flavor to develop, so be sure to plan in advance.

1 cup raw macadamia nuts, soaked 3–4 hours and drained

⅓ cup + 1 Tablespoon water

2 Tablespoons nutritional yeast

1 clove garlic, quartered

2 teaspoons lemon juice

½ teaspoon salt

35–40 small cremini mushrooms, stems removed

⅓ cup soy sauce (use tamari for gluten-free option)

Thinly sliced lettuce ribbons for serving

The day before serving:
Place nuts, water, nutritional yeast, garlic and lemon juice in a high-powered blender and process until very smooth (you may need to scrape down the sides once or twice while blending). Add salt and process for another 10 seconds. Place filling in a small bowl and cover with a clean towel. Let the filling rest overnight at room temperature (or at least 8 hours prior to serving).

About an hour before you're ready to serve:
Place mushrooms and soy sauce in a large bowl. Carefully use a rubber spatula to toss the mushrooms around, coating them with sauce. Let mushrooms marinate for up to an hour, tossing occasionally to ensure that each mushroom is evenly marinated.

APPETIZERS & SNACKS

Place lettuce onto a medium serving platter in an even layer. Arrange mushrooms on platter, being sure to drain off any excess soy sauce as you remove each one from the bowl. Transfer macadamia filling into a pastry bag, then pipe filling into each mushroom and serve immediately.

APPETIZERS & SNACKS

SERVES
4–6

PREP TIME
5 minutes

TOTAL TIME
5 minutes
+ cooking beans

CLASSIC HUMMUS

If you're accustomed to buying hummus at the store, you'll find that making your own is both more delicious and friendlier on your food budget. I love making variations that deviate from the traditional garbanzo/tahini combo (as you'll see in the following two recipes), but you can never go wrong with the classic version here.

2 cups cooked garbanzo beans*

1 cup reserved garbanzo cooking liquid or water

½ cup tahini

¼ cup lemon juice

2 cloves garlic, quartered

1 teaspoon ground cumin

¾ teaspoon salt

Place all ingredients except salt in a food processor, being sure to start with just a ½ cup of garbanzo liquid or water (you'll be able to add more later if you wish).

Process well, scraping down the sides as needed. For a smoother/thinner hummus, or to aid in processing if needed, add additional garbanzo liquid or water, a tablespoon at a time. When the desired texture is reached, add in salt and process for another 20–30 seconds. Taste and adjust seasonings as you wish. Refrigerate hummus in a sealed container until ready to serve.

As a general rule, dried garbanzos will roughly triple in volume when cooked. So, for this recipe, use 2/3 cup dried garbanzos (or use 2 cans of garbanzos).

APPETIZERS & SNACKS

ROASTED BUTTERNUT SQUASH HUMMUS

SERVES
4–6

PREP TIME
10 minutes

COOK TIME
25 minutes

TOTAL TIME
25 minutes
+ cooking beans
+ cooling

The idea for this hummus was born when I needed to make something for a potluck and was determined to use a container of leftover roasted butternut squash and a partial can of coconut milk that were in my refrigerator. The coconut milk replaces tahini in this variation, which together with the squash gives the hummus a delightfully sweet tinge.

1½ cups butternut squash, peeled and cubed

1 teaspoon olive oil

2 cups cooked garbanzo beans (see note on opposite page)

1 cup full-fat coconut milk

2 cloves garlic, quartered

1½ teaspoons Ras el Hanout*

1 teaspoon salt

Preheat oven to 375 degrees.

Toss squash with olive oil and bake for 20–25 minutes, until tender. Let squash cool before making hummus. (This step can be done a day or two in advance if needed.)

Add cooled squash and all other ingredients except salt to a food processor. Process well, scraping down the sides as needed. When the desired texture is reached, add in salt and process for another 20–30 seconds. Taste and adjust seasonings as you wish. Refrigerate hummus in a sealed container until ready to serve.

Ras el Hanout is a spice blend from Morocco that is traditionally a combination of at least a dozen spices (if not far more – I bought one in the medina of Fez that had a whopping 45 in it). It is now fairly easy to find commercially, including at Whole Foods Markets and from specialty spice retailers.

APPETIZERS & SNACKS

SERVES
4–6

PREP TIME
5 minutes

TOTAL TIME
5 minutes
+ cooking lentils

BLACK LENTIL HUMMUS

This is a great hummus for people who have trouble digesting garbanzos, and is also perhaps a better choice for parties, since lentils tend to be less gas-inducing. The color of this hummus is striking, and its spicy cayenne punch is equally bold.

2½ cups cooked black lentils (sometimes also sold as beluga lentils)*

½ cup lemon juice

⅓ cup tahini

¼ cup olive oil

1 clove garlic, quartered

1 teaspoon ground cumin

⅛–¼ teaspoon cayenne pepper (use more or less to your taste)

1 teaspoon salt

Place all ingredients except salt in a food processor. Process well, scraping down the sides as needed. When the desired texture is reached, add in salt and process for another 20–30 seconds. Taste and adjust seasonings as you wish. Refrigerate hummus in a sealed container until ready to serve.

Black lentils roughly double in size when cooked, so begin with about 1¼ cup dried lentils. If you have any extras, they can be sprinkled on top as a garnish. Lentils can be cooked in advance and refrigerated until ready to use.

APPETIZERS & SNACKS

APPETIZERS & SNACKS

SERVES
4–6

PREP TIME
10 minutes

COOK TIME
15 minutes

TOTAL TIME
25 minutes
+ overnight chill

CURRIED RED LENTIL DIP

This simple dip is a great appetizer to serve with sliced veggies or chips as part of an Indian-inspired feast. It also stores well and can be kept in the refrigerator for a go-to snack throughout the week.

2 cups dried red lentils

2 teaspoons ghee (or coconut oil for vegan option)

1 large red onion, diced

2 Tablespoons curry powder

1 teaspoon salt

Bring 4 cups of water to a boil, add the red lentils, and cook for about 15 minutes at a simmer until lentils are soft. Drain, allow lentils to cool, and refrigerate overnight (the texture of the dip is much better if you process them when cool).

The next day, heat ghee/oil in a medium skillet and add the onion. Cook over low heat for about half an hour until onions are soft and caramelized, stirring occasionally. Let them cool slightly before proceeding.

Place chilled lentils, cooked onions, and curry powder in a food processor, and process until desired texture is achieved, scraping down the sides as needed. (Add a tablespoon or two of water if needed to help processing.) Store dip in a sealed container in the refrigerator until ready to serve.

ARUGULA & ARTICHOKE DIP

SERVES
4–6

PREP TIME
10 minutes

TOTAL TIME
10 minutes

I have a friend who grows the tastiest arugula ever in his backyard garden. I once received several pounds and was searching for all kinds of creative ways to use it, thus inspiring this recipe. Think of it as a more refined, grown-up take on the commonplace spinach and artichoke dip (without the junk you'd find in the deli counter version). In my home, we sometimes treat this dip like a pesto and eat it over pasta.

⅓ cup pumpkin seeds

1 clove garlic, quartered

2 Tablespoons lemon juice

1 can artichoke hearts in water, drained

2-4 ounces arugula (more for a peppery taste, less for mild flavor)

1 Tablespoon olive oil (optional)

¼ cup nutritional yeast

½ teaspoon salt

Place pumpkin seeds in a food processor and pulse a few times until seeds are coarsely ground. Add in garlic and lemon juice and pulse a few more times until garlic is also coarsely chopped.

Add in artichoke hearts, arugula and olive oil (if using). Run food processor until artichokes are chopped and slightly creamy, scraping down the sides as needed. Add in nutritional yeast and salt and run the machine for anadditional 20–30 seconds. Store dip in a sealed container in the refrigerator until ready to serve.

APPETIZERS & SNACKS

SERVES
4–6

PREP TIME
15 minutes

COOK TIME
12–18 hours

TOTAL TIME
12+ hours

ZESTY KALE CHIPS

I hate to break it to you, but the only truly good way to make kale chips is in a dehydrator. If you've been reluctant to purchase one, this recipe alone justifies the investment, especially if you are someone who buys tiny bags of kale chips at $8 a pop. Craigslist, eBay and other secondhand retailers are often full of bargains on dehydrators (including some that have never even been used), so look around if you want to get a good deal on one.

2 large bunches green curly kale, de-ribbed and torn into small pieces

1 cup raw cashews, soaked at least 2–3 hours and drained

¾ cup water

¼ cup lemon juice

¼ cup nutritional yeast

1 teaspoon salt

Place prepared kale in a very large mixing bowl.

Add all remaining ingredients except salt to a high-speed blender and process until very smooth. Add in salt and process for another 10–15 seconds.

Scrape the cashew sauce into the bowl with the kale and use your hands to spread the sauce evenly over it. Divide the saucy kale onto two or more dehydrator sheets (the exact number you need will vary by machine), using liner sheets if you have them. Be sure that the kale is in a single layer.

Dehydrate chips for 12–18 hours, until coating is hardened and chips are crunchy. Again, exact timing will vary by machine. If your dehydrator has a temperature selector, choose 115 degrees.

Store kale chips in tightly-sealed jars or containers.

APPETIZERS & SNACKS

·· OTHER FLAVOR COMBINATIONS TO TRY ··

Add ⅓ cup chopped red bell pepper

· · · · · · · ·

Add 1 small chipotle chile

· · · · · · · ·

Add a large handful of basil

· · · · · · · ·

Add a couple cloves of garlic

· · · · · · · ·

APPETIZERS & SNACKS

SERVES
3–4

PREP TIME
10 minutes

TOTAL TIME
10 minutes

GUACAMOLE THREE WAYS

As a native Texan, I can't live without good guacamole. There is no such thing as a good packaged guacamole in my experience, so it is always worth making your own. Here is my go-to recipe, along with two fun variations to explore.

3 medium ripe avocados

2 small tomatoes, diced

¼ cup red onion, finely diced

Juice of one lime (plus extra for storage)

Large handful of chopped cilantro (optional)

¼ teaspoon salt

Use a spoon to scrape all avocado meat into a medium mixing bowl, then use a potato masher or large fork to mash it well. It should not be totally smooth, so don't go overboard.

Add in all remaining ingredients and stir well. Taste and add more lime juice and/or salt as you wish. Serve immediately, or store in refrigerator for later use. To best store guacamole, place in a container and sprinkle a thin coating of lime juice over the surface. Press parchment or plastic wrap over the guacamole so that it makes contact, then seal with a lid and refrigerate.

APPETIZERS & SNACKS

· · OTHER FLAVOR COMBINATIONS TO TRY · ·
· MANGO JALAPEÑO GUACAMOLE ·

*Follow basic recipe, but add 1 cubed mango in place of the tomatoes.
Add up to one whole very-finely-diced jalapeño with seeds removed
(unless you enjoy things very spicy, in which case feel free to leave the seeds in!)*

· · · · · · · ·

· COOLING CUCUMBER GUACAMOLE ·

*Follow basic recipe, but omit tomatoes and include one small cucumber
(diced) in their place. Leave out onion as well, and feel free to add additional
cilantro for extra cooling.*

· · · · · · · ·

APPETIZERS & SNACKS

MAKES
1 large bowl

COOK TIME
5 minutes

TOTAL TIME
5 minutes

GARAM MASALA POPCORN

A favorite restaurant of mine in Chicago used to serve a version of this as a tasty amuse-bouche. Being a huge popcorn fan, I quickly set about recreating the recipe and hope you'll enjoy it as much as I do. The spices in the garam masala add flavor (and some medicinal value) to a snack that is otherwise pretty plain.

1 Tablespoon coconut oil

⅓ cup popcorn kernels

2 teaspoons garam masala*

Salt

Melt coconut oil in a fairly large heavy-bottomed pot (that has a tight-fitting lid) over medium heat. Stir in popcorn kernels and garam masala, and stir to coat kernels well. Place the lid on the pan and listen for popping to begin.

Once popping has commenced, carefully shake the pot every 20 seconds or so and return it to the stove. Once there are at least 3-4 seconds between pops, turn off heat and give the pot a final shake. Keep covered for an additional 20 seconds so any last kernels can pop, then carefully remove lid and pour popcorn into a bowl. Season with salt to taste and eat immediately. Popcorn can also be stored in sealed glass jars once cool.

*Garam masala is a popular Indian spice blend. You can make your own (see p. 216) or purchase it.

THE SKINNY ON SALT

One of the most common questions I get asked is what salt I recommend using. There are a number of factors to consider when choosing salt, including the distance it had to travel to reach your plate. For this reason, my go-to salt is Redmond's Real Salt, easily found in many markets and online. Real Salt is sourced in Utah, so unlike some other popular salts, it has not traveled around the world and, thus, has a reduced carbon footprint. It also has a beautiful multi-tone pink hue to it because of all the various minerals it contains and comes in a few varieties. If you are in the U.S., I highly recommend it. If not, I suggest finding a salt that is sourced as locally as possible. Any good sea salt will do.

Himalayan pink salt has become very popular in recent years but can be problematic because it is sometimes cut using metal blades made of nickel and other metals that are not recommended for frequent consumption.

The one salt I certainly do not recommend using is the white table salt with which many of us grew up. In addition to being stripped of its naturally occurring trace minerals, it often contains unnecessary additives to keep it from clumping. Many of us have been led to believe table salt is advantageous because it is iodized, but it if you are eating a robust variety of natural foods in your diet, I can assure you with great confidence that you are getting enough iodine from your food alone.

The size of the salt crystals also makes a difference, so always choose an average size salt (think about the size of normal table salt crystals). Super fine salts will generally make foods taste saltier, so use them in reduced amounts if that is all you have on hand. Coarser salts, like kosher salt, are good for massaging into raw foods that will then be rinsed and for other specific purposes, but I do not advocate using them in everyday cooking.

Whenever you are adding salt to a mechanically-blended recipe (whether you are using a conventional blender, immersion blender, or a food processor), salt should always be added after or at the very end of the blending. The powerful blade of the machine will grind up your salt crystals, rendering them much smaller and giving a more salty taste to your finished product.

The most important thing with salt is always to taste foods as you cook and adjust the salt accordingly. All the salt measurements you will find here or in any recipe should always be seen as rough guidelines, but you, as the chef, should always make the final call.

SOUPS

COCONUT FENNEL CHOWDER

CHILLED CUCUMBER & AVOCADO SOUP

BUTTERNUT SQUASH, FUJI APPLE & CHIPOTLE SOUP

COCONUT CURRY LENTIL SOUP

LEBANESE LENTIL SOUP

SMOKY POTATO LEEK SOUP

MOROCCAN ACORN SQUASH & PEAR SOUP

MOROCCAN HARIRA

CUCUMBER YOGURT MINT SOUP

MISO SOUP WITH VEGETABLES & ALMONDS

RUSTIC WATERMELON GAZPACHO

ASPARAGUS, WATERCRESS & CAULIFLOWER SOUP

SOUPS

SERVES
4

PREP TIME
15 minutes

COOK TIME
35 minutes

TOTAL TIME
50 minutes

COCONUT FENNEL CHOWDER

Coconut milk replaces dairy products to give this soup a silky, creamy texture. If you eat fish, you can add cod or other white fish for a hearty stew.

1 small onion, sliced into quarter moons

1 pound fennel bulbs (no stalks), halved and thinly sliced

1½ teaspoons olive oil

2 russet potatoes, peeled and cut into ¾-inch cubes

3 cups vegetable broth

One 15-ounce can full-fat coconut milk

2 Tablespoons chopped fennel fronds

1 teaspoon salt

Preheat oven to 375 degrees.

Toss onion and fennel with olive oil and spread onto a large baking sheet in a single layer. Roast for 15–20 minutes or until edges are lightly browned, flipping once halfway through cooking.

While veggies roast, place the potato in a small saucepan and cover with water. Bring potato to a boil over high heat, then simmer over a lower flame for 4–5 minutes or until outside of potato is just fork-tender. Drain potato and set aside.

Place about two-thirds of the roasted fennel and onion mixture in a large saucepan or small stockpot, along with half the potato. Add the broth and coconut milk and use an immersion blender to puree everything until very smooth. Alternatively, place everything in a conventional blender and puree, and then transfer to a pot.

Add the remaining roasted vegetables and potato to the pureed mixture along with the fennel fronds. Heat soup over a medium flame and simmer for 10–15 minutes or until potato is fully cooked. Stir in salt and adjust to taste as needed. Serve soup immediately or keep covered until ready to serve.

CHILLED CUCUMBER & AVOCADO SOUP

SERVES
2

PREP TIME
10 minutes

TOTAL TIME
10 minutes
+ chilling

This soup is the perfect start to a summertime dinner party. Be sure to let it chill before serving for the best flavor.

1 pound cucumbers, halved lengthwise and chopped into ½-inch pieces

1 large avocado (or 2 small avocados)

Juice of 2–3 limes

¾ cup coconut water

1 teaspoon salt

Dash of cayenne pepper (optional)

Lime slices for serving

Place all ingredients except salt in a blender, and process until smooth. Add additional coconut water or filtered water if needed to achieve desired consistency. Add salt and process an additional 20 seconds. Adjust salt or cayenne as desired. Chill soup for 1–2 hours in the refrigerator before serving.

Serve in individual bowls garnished with lime slices.

BUTTERNUT SQUASH, FUJI APPLE & CHIPOTLE SOUP

SERVES 6

PREP TIME 20 minutes

COOK TIME 50 minutes

TOTAL TIME 1 hour 10 minutes

This soup was created on a cold winter day when I was feeling both jet-lagged and heartbroken. It's been a staple in my menus ever since and always leaves me feeling comforted.

1 Tablespoon ghee (or olive oil for a vegan option)

1 red onion, chopped

2 leeks (white portions only), thinly sliced

2 pounds butternut squash, peeled, seeded and chopped

2 Fuji apples, peeled, cored and chopped

6 cups vegetable broth

1–2 chipotle chiles in adobo sauce

1 teaspoon salt

Heat ghee/oil in a large saucepan or small stockpot over medium heat. Add red onion and cook until translucent. Reduce heat and cook for 10–15 minutes, stirring occasionally, until onion begins to caramelize. Add leeks and cook for 3–4 minutes or until leeks are soft.

Add butternut squash, apples and vegetable broth. Raise heat to high, bring to a boil, and then reduce to a simmer. Cook soup covered for 20–25 minutes or until squash is fork-tender.

Add chipotle chiles and then use an immersion blender to puree soup until smooth and velvety. Alternatively, use a conventional blender to puree soup in batches and transfer soup back to the pot. Stir in salt and cook soup for an additional 5 minutes to let flavors meld. Serve soup immediately or keep covered until ready to serve.

SOUPS

SOUPS

SERVES
4

PREP TIME
15 minutes

COOK TIME
40 minutes

TOTAL TIME
55 minutes

COCONUT CURRY LENTIL SOUP

This recipe was inspired by a soup I used to eat at the Berkeley Bowl, a beloved grocery store where I used to have lunch dates every Friday while I was a graduate student.

2 teaspoons ghee (or olive oil for a vegan option)

1 onion, diced

1½ cups red lentils, rinsed

2 carrots, quartered lengthwise and chopped

2 russet potatoes, peeled and cubed

2 tablespoons curry powder*

3½ cups vegetable broth

One 15-ounce can coconut milk

1 teaspoon salt

Heat ghee/oil in a large saucepan or small stockpot over medium heat. Add onion and cook until translucent, about 5-6 minutes. Add lentils, carrots, potatoes and curry powder and cook for 1-2 minutes, stirring often.

Add vegetable broth and bring soup to a boil over high heat. Reduce heat to a simmer and cook covered, stirring occasionally, for 20-25 minutes or until potatoes are fork-tender.

Add coconut milk and salt. Stir well and cook soup for an additional 5 minutes. Adjust curry powder/salt to taste. Serve soup immediately or keep covered until ready to serve.

*Choose a Vadouvan variety of curry powder if you can find it; otherwise, any curry blend will do.

SOUPS

LEBANESE LENTIL SOUP

SERVES 6

My take on this staple Middle Eastern soup includes cumin, coriander and lots of fresh mint. These ingredients add a ton of flavor and also aid digestion.

PREP TIME 15 minutes

COOK TIME 40 minutes

TOTAL TIME 55 minutes

2 teaspoons olive oil

1 large onion, diced

2 cloves garlic, minced

2 carrots, diced

2 stalks celery, diced

1 Tablespoon ground cumin

1 Tablespoon ground coriander

2 cups brown lentils

6 cups vegetable broth

Juice of one lemon

1 large handful fresh mint leaves, chopped

1 handful parsley, chopped

1½ teaspoons salt

Additional mint and parsley for serving

Heat oil in a large saucepan or small stockpot over medium heat. Add onion and cook until soft, about 5-6 minutes. Stir in garlic and cook until fragrant, about 30 seconds. Add in carrots and celery and cook an for additional 4-5 minutes. Add cumin and coriander and stir to coat vegetables with spices. Add in the lentils and broth. Raise heat to high, bring to a boil, and then reduce to a simmer. Cook soup covered for 25-30 minutes or until lentils are tender.

Just before serving, stir in the lemon juice, fresh herbs and salt. Adjust soup to taste, adding in more spices, lemon juice or salt as desired. Serve soup immediately, garnished with additional fresh herbs.

SOUPS

SERVES
6

PREP TIME
15 minutes

COOK TIME
55 minutes

TOTAL TIME
1 hour
10 minutes

SMOKY POTATO LEEK SOUP

Smoked paprika adds a delicious flavor twist to this classic soup and gives it a beautiful pink color as well.

1½ Tablespoons ghee (or olive oil for a vegan option)

1 onion, chopped

3 leeks (white portions only), thinly sliced

2 stalks celery, chopped

1 teaspoon fresh thyme

2 pounds russet potatoes, peeled and chopped

6 cups vegetable broth

1½ Tablespoons smoked paprika (plus extra for serving)

1 teaspoon salt

Chopped chives

Heat ghee/oil in a large saucepan or small stockpot over medium heat. Add onion and leeks and cook for 12-15 minutes or until vegetables begin to brown and caramelize. Add celery and thyme and cook for 3 minutes more.

Add potatoes and broth to cover the potatoes by about ¼" (use more liquid for a thinner soup). Raise heat to high, bring to a boil and then reduce to a simmer. Cook soup covered for 20-25 minutes or until potatoes are fork-tender.

Stir in smoked paprika and then use an immersion blender to puree soup until smooth. Alternatively, use a conventional blender to puree soup in batches and transfer soup back to the pot. Stir in salt and cook soup for an additional 5-10 minutes. Serve soup immediately or keep covered until ready to serve. Garnish individual servings with additional smoked paprika and chopped chives.

SOUPS

SERVES
6

PREP TIME
15 minutes

COOK TIME
1 hour 20 minutes

TOTAL TIME
1 hour
35 minutes

MOROCCAN ACORN SQUASH & PEAR SOUP

Although this soup is not a traditional Moroccan preparation, it exemplifies the way that Moroccans expertly blend sweet and savory flavors in their cuisine.

2 acorn squash, halved and seeded

2 Tablespoons olive oil, divided

2 cloves garlic, halved

1 onion, chopped

1 leek (white portions only), thinly sliced

2 pears, peeled and diced

6 cups vegetable broth

1½ teaspoons Ras el Hanout

1 teaspoon salt

Preheat oven to 400 degrees.

Place prepared acorn squash on a parchment-lined baking tray, skin side down. Brush squash with 1 tablespoon of the olive oil and place a piece of garlic inside each squash half. Bake squash for 45 minutes or until very tender. Remove from oven and let squash cool for about 20 minutes or until cool to the touch. Remove and reserve garlic and then use a spoon to scoop out all squash flesh into a bowl.

In a soup pot, heat the remaining 1 tablespoon of olive oil over medium heat. Add onion and leeks and sauté until they begin to brown, about 7–8 minutes. Add squash, garlic, pear and vegetable broth. Raise heat to high, bring to a boil and then reduce to a simmer. Cook soup covered for 10 minutes.

Stir in Ras el Hanout and then use an immersion blender to puree soup until smooth. Alternatively, use a conventional blender to puree soup in batches and transfer soup back to the pot. Stir in salt and cook soup for an additional 5–10 minutes. Serve soup immediately or keep covered until ready to serve.

MOROCCAN HARIRA

This soup is traditionally eaten in Morocco and other North African countries after each day of fasting for the Ramadan holiday. Do not skip serving this soup with dates—the flavor combination is divine!

G V

SERVES 4

PREP TIME 10 minutes

COOK TIME 1 hour

TOTAL TIME 1 hour 10 minutes

1½ teaspoons olive oil

1 small onion, diced

1 clove garlic, minced

2 teaspoons sweet paprika

1 teaspoon ground ginger

½ teaspoon turmeric powder

½ teaspoon ground cinnamon

¼ teaspoon saffron, crumbled

¼ teaspoon ground black pepper

One 28-ounce can diced tomatoes (with liquid)

⅔ cup red lentils, rinsed

1¼ teaspoons salt

½ cup vermicelli or angel hair pasta, broken into inch-long pieces (gluten-free if needed)

Lemon wedges and halved dates for serving

Heat oil in a large saucepan or small stockpot over medium heat. Add the onion and cook for 5-6 minutes or until soft. Stir in garlic, all spices and tomatoes. Cook until mixture begins to simmer and then add red lentils and 4 cups of water. Turn heat to high and bring to a boil, stirring occasionally. Once boiling, reduce heat to low, partially cover with a lid left ajar and cook for 45 minutes or until tomatoes and lentils are very soft.

Remove pot from heat and use an immersion blender to puree soup until smooth. Alternatively, use a conventional blender to puree soup in batches and transfer soup back to the pot. Return pot to the stove over medium heat, and add the salt and vermicelli. Cook for another 5 minutes, stirring often to prevent noodles from sticking to the bottom of the pot. Adjust salt as needed and then serve in individual bowls accompanied by a lemon wedge and two date halves.

CUCUMBER YOGURT MINT SOUP

SERVES
3

PREP TIME
10 minutes

TOTAL TIME
10 minutes

This easy blender soup is my take on a traditional Persian soup. It is most enjoyable when eaten the same day it is made.

⅔ cup water

⅓ cup lemon or lime juice

1 cup plain yogurt (use coconut yogurt for a vegan option)

2 large cucumbers, peeled, seeded and chopped

15–20 mint leaves (plus extra for garnish)

¾ teaspoon salt

Place all ingredients in a blender in the order listed, except for the salt. Process at a high speed until smooth and creamy. Add salt and process for 10-20 seconds at a low speed. Serve immediately or keep chilled until ready to serve. Garnish individual servings with mint leaves.

SERVES 6

PREP TIME 20 minutes

COOK TIME 50 minutes

TOTAL TIME 1 hour 10 minutes

MISO SOUP WITH VEGETABLES & ALMONDS

People are always surprised when they eat this soup and experience a crunchy bite. I got the idea of adding almonds from a friend years ago and have never left them out of my miso soup since then.

1 medium sweet potato, peeled and chopped

1½ teaspoons sunflower oil

1 small onion, thinly sliced into quarter moons

1 stalk celery, chopped

1 carrot, quartered lengthwise and chopped

1 small daikon radish, quartered lengthwise and chopped

1 cup sliced mushrooms (I like to use shiitakes)

5 cups vegetable broth

2 Tablespoons dried wakame seaweed*

¼ cup raw almonds (unsalted)

1 Tablespoon soy sauce (or use tamari for a gluten-free option)

2 Tablespoons miso paste

Salt to taste

Place sweet potato in a small saucepan and add just enough water to cover. Bring to a boil over high heat, then cover and cook for 20 minutes over a low flame or until very tender.

While sweet potato cooks, heat oil in a large saucepan or small stockpot over medium heat. Add the onion and sauté for 2–3 minutes or until it just begins to soften. Add celery, carrot, daikon radish and mushrooms, and sauté for 4–5 minutes or until mushrooms are shiny. Add broth and turn flame to high until soup boils.

Reduce heat to medium-low and simmer for 15 minutes. Then add in wakame, almonds and tamari soy sauce and cook for another 10 minutes. Add the miso to the sweet potato and its cooking water, and then blend together using either an immersion blender or a whisk. Stir the sweet potato-miso mixture into the soup and cook for an additional 5 minutes. Taste soup and add salt as desired. Serve immediately or keep covered until ready to serve.

If your wakame comes in large strips, use kitchen scissors to cut it into very small pieces. It will expand significantly once it is cooked

HANDLE WITH CARE

When making miso soup, always be mindful to keep the temperature on the stove very low once the miso has been added. Miso is a living food full of beneficial probiotic microbes that contain enzymes that aid in digestion and support gut health. At high temperatures, these delicate organisms die and lose their potency, so avoid boiling or simmering the soup once the miso has been added. This also goes for leftovers—always reheat them very gently!

I love using miso in dressings and sauces where heat is not an issue. Avoid recipes that call for roasting or baking foods with miso, or just be aware that while the flavor of miso may be present, its health benefits will be greatly diminished.

SOUPS

SERVES
4

PREP TIME
20 minutes

TOTAL TIME
20 minutes
+ chilling

RUSTIC WATERMELON GAZPACHO

Rustic gazpachos are traditionally prepared to be chunkier than the silky smooth varieties you may have experienced. This soup is perfect for mid- to late-summer, when tomatoes and melons are at their peaks.

4 cups seedless watermelon, peeled and cubed

2 heirloom tomatoes, chopped

½ cucumber, peeled, seeded and chopped

½ bell pepper, seeded and chopped

½ red onion, chopped

1 Tablespoon sherry vinegar

1 Tablespoon good-quality olive oil

¼ teaspoon salt

Thin watermelon slices for serving

Place watermelon in a blender or food processor and process on high speed until it begins to liquefy. Add all remaining ingredients and process at a low speed for 20–30 seconds until the veggies are finely chopped. Chill gazpacho for at least an hour, and adjust vinegar and salt as desired before serving. Serve in individual bowls, garnished with watermelon slices.

SOUPS

SERVES
6

PREP TIME
20 minutes

COOK TIME
1 hour

TOTAL TIME
1 hour
20 minutes

ASPARAGUS, WATERCRESS & CAULIFLOWER SOUP

This soup is springtime captured in a bowl. It is extremely nutrient dense, in part thanks to watercress, a small but mighty green vegetable that is loaded with vitamins and minerals (including more calcium than milk!).

1 small head cauliflower, chopped into large florets

3 Tablespoons olive oil, divided

1 small onion, chopped

1 leek (white portion only), thinly sliced

1 clove garlic, minced

¾ pound bunch of asparagus, chopped into 1-inch pieces

½ cup raw cashews, soaked minimum 2 hours and drained

4 cups vegetable broth

2 tablespoons chopped parsley

1 bunch watercress, roots removed and roughly chopped

Salt and pepper

Preheat oven to 400 degrees.

In a large bowl, toss cauliflower with 1 tablespoon of olive oil. Spread on a baking sheet and season lightly with salt and pepper. Roast cauliflower in the oven for 30 minutes, or until edges are lightly browned, flipping halfway through cooking. Let cauliflower cool while you proceed with the remaining steps.

Heat remaining oil in a large saucepan or small stockpot over medium heat. Add onion and leeks and sauté until translucent and soft, about 5-6 minutes. Add garlic and cook for another minute. Stir in asparagus and roasted cauliflower, and cook 2 minutes before adding soaked cashews and broth. Raise heat to high, bring to a boil and then reduce heat to a simmer. Cook soup covered for 20–25 minutes or until asparagus and cauliflower are very tender.

Turn heat off and then add parsley and watercress. Stir until leaves wilt slightly and then use an immersion blender to puree soup until smooth. Alternatively, use a conventional blender to puree soup in batches and transfer soup back to the pot. Turn heat to low and stir in ¾ teaspoon salt. Cook soup another 5 minutes and then serve.*

*This soup will lose its beautiful green color if left to sit, so I recommend preparing it just before eating.

MAINS

RAW TACOS

LENTIL SHEPHERD'S PIE

COLLARD WRAPS WITH
SHIITAKE-SUNFLOWER SEED PÂTÉ

JACKFRUIT FESENJAN

BEETLOAF

KITCHARI

ZUCCHINI WALNUT PASTA

BUTTERNUT SQUASH & SAGE RISOTTO

GRILLED CAULIFLOWER STEAKS WITH HARISSA

MOROCCAN VEGETABLE TAGINE

BAKED ZUCCHINI BOATS

CREAMY DIJON TEMPEH

MAINS

SERVES
4

PREP TIME
20 minutes

TOTAL TIME
20 minutes

RAW TACOS

These kid-friendly tacos make a great no-cook meal that can be prepped in advance and assembled just before eating. The walnut and sundried tomato filling can also be used in traditional tacos as a substitute for meat.

½ cup sundried tomatoes (not oil-packed)

1½ cups raw walnuts

2 teaspoons ground cumin

1 teaspoon chile powder

½ teaspoon salt

2 heads Little Gems or other petite lettuce

Chipotle cashew cream (see p. 197)

Toppings of your choice (diced tomato, avocado, etc.)

Place sundried tomatoes in a small bowl and cover with boiling water. Let tomatoes sit for 5 minutes and then drain, being sure to reserve soaking water. Rinse tomatoes with cool water and then chop roughly.

Place prepared tomatoes, walnuts, cumin and chile powder in a food processor, along with 1/3 cup of tomato soaking liquid. Process until a crumbly filling that roughly resembles ground meat is achieved. Add salt and process for 20 seconds, then taste and adjust seasonings as desired. Store filling in a sealed container until ready to serve.

To assemble tacos, place individual lettuce leaves on a serving platter and then spoon filling into each. Garnish with cashew chipotle cream and other toppings and then serve.

MAINS

SERVES
6

PREP TIME
45 minutes

COOK TIME
25 minutes

TOTAL TIME
1 hour
10 minutes

LENTIL SHEPHERD'S PIE

For me, shepherd's pie is the ultimate comfort food and well worth the effort it takes to prepare. The various components of this recipe can be prepped in advance and assembled just before baking if you are short on time.

1¼ cups French green lentils

2 pounds sweet potatoes, peeled and roughly chopped

3 Tablespoons olive oil, divided

1 small onion, finely diced

1 small carrot, cut into small dice

2 stalks celery, cut into small dice

6 mushrooms, cut into small dice

½ small zucchini, cut into small dice

¼ cup all-purpose flour (use brown rice flour for gluten-free option)

2 Tablespoons + 1 teaspoon soy sauce (use tamari for gluten-free option)

½ teaspoon fresh thyme, chopped

1 teaspoon salt

Place lentils and 3 cups of water in a medium pot. Bring to a boil over high heat, then cover and reduce heat to low. Cook for about 20 minutes until lentils are tender but still keep their shape. Drain any excess water, and let lentils cool slightly.

While lentils cool, prepare the sweet potato topping, vegetables and gravy:
Place sweet potatoes in a medium pot and add just enough water to cover them. Bring to a boil over high heat, then cover and reduce heat to low. Cook for 12–15 minutes or until very tender, then drain excess water and return them to the pot. Lightly season potatoes with salt and then use a potato masher to mash them well. Don't worry about small lumps, as these will be smoothed out in the assembly stage. Cover pot and set aside.

In a medium skillet, heat 1 tablespoon of olive oil, then add onion and cook 1-2 minutes until it begins turning translucent. Add remaining diced vegetables and cook for another 4-5 minutes. Turn off heat and set aside.

In a small saucepan, heat the remaining 2 tablespoons of olive oil over medium heat. Stir in the flour and continue stirring for about two minutes, until mixture begins to turn golden. Combine soy sauce and 1¼ cups water in a small bowl, then whisk into the flour roux. Once all lumps are dissolved, raise the heat slightly and continue whisking gravy until it boils. When boiling, stir in the thyme and reduce heat to low. Cook 3-4 minutes longer to allow gravy to thicken, then remove from heat.

Assembly:
Preheat oven to 375 degrees.

In a large bowl, stir together cooked lentils and vegetables, as well as the gravy and salt. Continue stirring until lentils are well coated with gravy. Taste the lentils, and add any additional salt as desired.

Spread lentil mixture into the bottom of a lightly oiled 8 x 8" baking dish (or other baking dish that is approximately 2 quarts), using a spatula to smooth it into an even layer. Then, use a spatula to spread the mashed sweet potato topping into a single even layer on top of the lentils. Be sure to spread the topping all the way to the edges of the pan to prevent gravy from bubbling up while baking. Bake for 25 minutes and then serve immediately. Use a large spoon for serving so that you can easily scoop up lentils as well as topping.

MAINS

SERVES
6

PREP TIME
25 minutes

TOTAL TIME
25 minutes
+ marinating

COLLARD WRAPS WITH SHIITAKE-SUNFLOWER SEED PÂTÉ

These wraps travel well and are always a hit wherever I bring them. They are also equally great as part of a meal or as a handheld party snack.

6 collard green leaves

2 Tablespoons lemon juice

¾ teaspoon salt

2 Tablespoons soy sauce (use tamari for gluten-free option)

6 medium shiitake mushrooms, chopped

2 cups sunflower seeds, soaked for at least 6 hours* and drained

2 Tablespoons white miso

3 scallions, trimmed and chopped (white and green parts)

Red or orange bell pepper, cut into thin strips

Clover sprouts or other delicate sprouts

Prepare wraps (8–12 hours before serving):
Use a knife to remove the ribs of the collard leaves. Place the 12 "wraps" in a shallow dish or plastic Ziploc bag. Mix together the lemon juice and salt, and pour it over the leaves, using your hands or a spoon to coat all leaves with the mixture. Allow wraps to marinate for 8–12 hours in the refrigerator before assembling wraps.

Prepare pâté:
Place shiitakes and soy sauce in a small bowl. Marinate mushrooms for 15–20 minutes, then place mushrooms and excess soy sauce in a food processor along with drained sunflower seeds, miso and scallion. Process until a smooth spread is achieved. Add 1 tablespoon of water to aid processing if required. Refrigerate pâté until ready to use.

Wrap assembly:

Place one collard wrap face down on a clean cutting board or other smooth surface, with the cut edge toward you. Use a small spoon to place about 2-3 tablespoons of pâté on the leaf, about 1½ inches from the right edge of the leaf. Use the spoon or your fingers to carefully form the pâté into a small log from the top to bottom edge of the leaf.

Place one strip of bell pepper toward the top of the log so that it sticks out above the top edge of the leaf, and add a small pinch of sprouts to the top as well. Roll the wrap up from right to left. The collard green should wrap around the pâté a maximum of two times, so if you have a larger leaf, use a knife to trim off any excess. Serve wraps immediately or place on a covered platter and refrigerate until ready to serve.

* Sunflower seeds can be soaked longer or sprouted

MAINS

SERVES
4

PREP TIME
15 minutes

COOK TIME
30 minutes

TOTAL TIME
45 minutes

JACKFRUIT FESENJAN

Fesenjan is a Persian pomegranate and walnut stew that is traditionally made with chicken. In my version, I use young jackfruit to create a stew that is just as hearty and satisfying as the original. If you're unable to find jackfruit, you could substitute garbanzo beans in its place.

2 cups walnuts

2 teaspoons olive oil

1 onion, sliced into half-moons

½ teaspoon turmeric powder

½ teaspoon ground cinnamon

Two 15-oz cans young jackfruit, drained*

1½ cups vegetable broth

⅓ cup pomegranate molasses**

2 Tablespoons maple syrup

¼ teaspoon salt

Cooked basmati rice (for serving)

Chopped parsley

Pomegranate arils (seeds), if available

Heat a large skillet over medium heat and add walnuts. Toast walnuts for 6–8 minutes until they are slightly browned and fragrant. Stir nuts occasionally and reduce heat as needed to prevent burning. Let walnuts cool slightly, then transfer them to a food processor and chop them into a fairly fine meal.

Heat oil in a Dutch oven or other heavy-bottomed pot over medium-high heat. Add onion and cook for 5–6 minutes or until soft. Stir in turmeric, cinnamon and jackfruit and cook for 1 minute. Add broth and bring to a boil. Lower heat and stir in ground walnuts, pomegranate molasses, maple syrup and salt. Cook for 20–25 minutes or until sauce has thickened. Taste and adjust salt as needed.

Serve fesenjan over individual servings of basmati rice, and garnish with parsley and pomegranate arils.

Jackfruit is a large prickly tropical fruit from Southern/Southeast Asia. In its unripe state, it is fairly neutral in flavor and can be used as a meat substitute. Several brands are now easily found in health food stores and Indian markets around the U.S. Try to find one that doesn't use preservatives and be sure not to buy ripened jackfruit in syrup.

**Pomegranate molasses is available at Middle Eastern markets or online, and in some more mainstream retail locations as well.*

MAINS

SERVES
6

PREP TIME
20 minutes

COOK TIME
55 minutes

TOTAL TIME
1 hour
15 minutes

BEETLOAF

I first discovered beetloaf at a diner in Albuquerque and was shocked to find such a delightful vegan option there. This is my own interpretation, filled with beets (of course) and packed with protein too. This recipe pairs well with the horseradish mashed potatoes found on p. 147.

¾ cup raw sunflower seeds (unsalted)

½ cup rolled oats (certified gluten-free if necessary)

½ pound mushrooms, coarsely chopped

1 cup cooked adzuki beans*

1½ cups (packed) grated beets

1 small onion, finely chopped

2 teaspoons tomato paste

2 teaspoons smoked paprika

1 teaspoon salt

Preheat oven to 375 degrees. Lightly oil a 9 x 5-inch loaf pan. (I recommend using a silicon pan for easiest removal.)

Place sunflower seeds, oats and mushrooms in a food processor and run until a crumbly uniform texture is achieved. Add in beans and pulse a few times to integrate them.

Place sunflower seed mixture in a large mixing bowl and add beet and onion. Stir well with a heavy wooden spoon. Once vegetables are mixed in, stir in tomato paste, smoked paprika and salt.

Transfer beetloaf mixture to the greased loaf pan, using a spatula to smooth the top evenly. Bake for 55-65 minutes, until the top is firm and just slightly crisp. Remove beetloaf from oven and let it cool for 8-10 minutes before slicing and serving.

To cook your own beans, you'll need to start with about 1/3 cup of dried beans. You can also substitute black beans or other prepared beans you may already have on hand.

MAINS

KITCHARI

SERVES
4

Kitchari is one of Ayurveda's most prized dishes, known for being both delicious and healing. Kitchari is extremely easy to digest and a great food to eat when you're under the weather, so it is sometimes referred to as "Indian chicken soup." Kitchari is commonly used as part of Ayurvedic cleansing regimens, and offers a food-based way to give your gut a mini vacation. I offer the option of adding vegetables to your kitchari for a complete one-pot meal.

PREP TIME
5 minutes

COOK TIME
40 minutes

TOTAL TIME
45 minutes

2 Tablespoons ghee (or coconut oil for vegan option)

1 teaspoon cumin seeds

1 teaspoon black mustard seeds

1-inch piece fresh ginger, peeled and grated

1 pinch hing, aka asafoetida (optional)

½ cup mung beans, soaked and drained*

¾ cup white basmati rice

4 cups water (use more for soupier kitchari)

¾ teaspoon turmeric powder

1-inch piece kombu seaweed (optional but recommended)

1 teaspoon salt

Up to 2 cups chopped vegetables (optional)

WHAT IS HING? Hing, more commonly known as *asafoetida* in the West, is a very pungent spice (note that its English moniker is derived from the word "fetid"!) that is quite common in Ayurvedic and Indian cooking. It is cultivated from the resin of a wild fennel plant that grows in certain parts of Asia and the Middle East. It has a unique pungent taste that is vaguely like garlic. Using hing can make foods that are somewhat hard to digest a bit easier and lead to less gas following a meal.

Hing has been listed as optional in all recipes in this book where it is called for, as some people really don't enjoy its flavor and/or smell. It is typically used in very sparse amounts (generally just a pinch at a time) so one jar goes a long way.

Heat ghee/oil in a medium pot over medium-low heat. Add cumin seeds, black mustard seeds, ginger and hing (if using), and sauté for a couple minutes until the mustard seeds begin to pop. Stir often to keep ginger from sticking to the bottom of the pot.

Stir in the drained mung beans and rice and cook for 2 minutes. Add water and raise the heat to high. Bring to a boil, then reduce heat back to medium low and stir in turmeric, kombu and salt. Cover and cook for 30–40 minutes or until rice and mung beans are soft. Stir occasionally as needed to prevent sticking.

If using fresh veggies, add the heartier veggies (like sweet potato or cauliflower) at the same time as the turmeric and kombu. Add lighter veggies (like greens) in the last 10 minutes of cooking. Serve kitchari with Cilantro Coconut Chutney or Mango Chutney (both found on p. 199), or enjoy on its own.

MAINS

MAINS

ZUCCHINI WALNUT PASTA

SERVES 4

PREP TIME 15 minutes

COOK TIME 10 minutes

TOTAL TIME 25 minutes

This summer dish is extremely simple to prepare and ready in a matter of minutes. You can play with adding additional flavors like chopped sundried tomatoes, olives or whatever else you may have on hand. Leftovers keep well and are great hot or cold.

1 pound fusilli pasta (gluten-free if necessary)

1 large zucchini, grated

⅛ cup chopped chives or scallion

½ cup chopped parsley (plus additional for garnish)

¼ cup good-quality olive oil

½ cup walnuts, finely chopped

1 teaspoon salt

¼ teaspoon fresh oregano, chopped

2 Tablespoons nutritional yeast (plus additional for garnish)

Dash of cayenne pepper (optional)

Cook pasta according to package instructions.

While pasta cooks, prepare all remaining ingredients and add to a large bowl. Stir well.

When pasta is ready, drain well in a colander and add it to the bowl with the zucchini mixture. Stir until pasta is well coated.

Serve immediately, garnished with extra parsley and/or nutritional yeast.

BUTTERNUT SQUASH & SAGE RISOTTO

SERVES 4

PREP TIME
15 minutes

COOK TIME
45 minutes

TOTAL TIME
1 hour

I always say that if you love someone, you should cook risotto for that person. The act of preparing risotto is one of the most loving culinary tasks I know of.

2 Tablespoons olive oil

1½ cups butternut squash, cut into ¾-inch cubes

4 cups vegetable broth

1 small onion, diced

2 cloves garlic, minced

2 Tablespoons fresh sage, chopped

1 cup Arborio rice

½ cup white wine (optional, or use an extra ½ cup of broth)

1 teaspoon dried sage

¼ cup nutritional yeast

1 teaspoon salt

Additional fresh sage or Italian parsley for garnish

Heat oven to 375 degrees. Toss butternut squash cubes with 1 tablespoon of olive oil, then place in a roasting pan or on a small baking sheet. Bake for 20 minutes, or until squash is tender but not mushy, and let it cool.

While the squash roasts, place the vegetable broth in a saucepan and warm it over medium-low heat.

In a medium-sized pot, heat the remaining 1 tablespoon of olive oil over medium-high heat, and add the onion and garlic. Cook until onion is fragrant and slightly translucent. Add the fresh sage and cook for 1 minute more.

Add the rice to the pot and stir constantly for 30 seconds. Add the white wine, if using, and continue stirring until it has been completely absorbed. Turn the heat off on the broth. Transfer broth to the rice pot (about a ½ cup at a time) using a ladle. Stir continuously and add the next batch of broth only after the previous batch has been almost completely absorbed.

Once all the broth has been added, stir in the dried sage, nutritional yeast and salt. Cook risotto for 5-10 minutes, until it has become somewhat thick and creamy. Gently fold in butternut squash, and adjust salt as needed. Serve immediately, or keep covered until ready to serve. Garnish individual portions with fresh sage or Italian parsley.

RISOTTO MEDITATION

With risotto, there are no shortcuts. If you do not actively stir the rice, the rice will not unleash its creamy essence, and you will likely end up with a burnt layer on the bottom of the pan.

I love making risotto precisely because it demands my full attention, allowing me to sink into a place of single focus. When I make risotto, I always carefully plan the rest of the menu so that I can have dedicated time to be at the stove, adding broth and stirring.

Instead of focusing on the time the process takes, I encourage you to focus instead on the opportunity you have to infuse love and well wishes into the food. You might even think of a mantra—a short affirmation of goodwill—and silently repeat that as you stir.

Like many things in life, a good risotto will take a chunk of time, but the results far outweigh the investment of energy that you will put in. Take the time to truly savor each bite, knowing the effort that went into the creation. I guarantee you will taste the love and intention you put in.

MAINS

SERVES
4

PREP TIME
45 minutes

COOK TIME
25 minutes

TOTAL TIME
1 hour
10 minutes

GRILLED CAULIFLOWER STEAKS WITH HARISSA

Fire up your grill and get ready to delight your taste buds. These sturdy steaks have flavor that will satisfy even the staunchest carnivore.

1 large head of cauliflower (or two smaller heads)

1 Tablespoon coriander seeds

⅓ cup olive oil

1 lemon, juiced and zested

1–2 cloves garlic, minced finely

1 Tablespoon smoked paprika

¾ teaspoon salt

Large handful of cilantro, chopped

Harissa (see p. 196)

Prepare cauliflower by trimming stem and any leaves. Place stem-side down on a cutting board, and slice cauliflower in half. Working from the flat side of each half outward, cut steaks that are about ¾-to 1-inch thick. Make sure both sides of each steak are perfectly flat and save any outer florets for another use.

Prepare marinade by whisking together all remaining ingredients (except cilantro) in a small bowl.

Heat your grill to medium. Brush one side of each steak with your marinade and place that side face-down on the grill. Cover the grill and cook for about 5 minutes, or until grill marks are present. Before flipping each steak, brush the top side with marinade, and then cook the second side for about the same amount of time as the first required.

Place finished steaks on a large serving platter and sprinkle cilantro over the steaks. Transfer harissa to a small serving bowl. Serve immediately.

MAINS

SERVES
6

PREP TIME
20 minutes

COOK TIME
40 minutes

TOTAL TIME
1 hour

AUTUMN VEGETABLE TAGINE

This filling Moroccan stew features warming spices and hearty grounding vegetables, perfect for cold days. It's great served over couscous or a grain of your choice, and can be enhanced with cooked beans or lentils for a more protein-rich option.

1½ Tablespoons coriander seeds

1½ teaspoons cumin seeds

2 teaspoons olive oil

1 large onion, sliced into thin half-moons

1 teaspoon ground cinnamon

½ teaspoon ground ginger

½ teaspoon saffron, soaked in 2 Tablespoons water

~4 cups chopped autumn vegetables, cut into small bite-sized pieces

1½ cups vegetable broth

¼ cup chopped dried apricots or prunes

Zest and juice of one lemon

1 teaspoon salt

Chopped parsley and/or cilantro, for garnish (optional)

Heat a small, heavy-bottomed skillet over a medium-high flame and add coriander and cumin seeds once hot. Cook for 1–2 minutes, stirring often, until the spices begin to emit an aroma. Turn off heat and transfer seeds to a spice grinder. After cooling for a couple of minutes, blend spices into a powder. (You may also use a mortar and pestle.)

Heat a large pot over medium-high heat and add olive oil, followed by the onion slices. Cook, stirring often, until onion begins to brown slightly, about 5–6 minutes. Stir in the cumin/coriander blend, along with the cinnamon, ginger and saffron as well as its soaking water. Add the chopped vegetables and broth and bring to a boil. Stir in the dried fruit and reduce heat to a very gentle simmer. Cook for 25–35 minutes, until vegetables are tender but not mushy.

Stir in lemon zest and juice, along with salt. Adjust the seasonings as you like. For a thicker tagine, let it cook for additional time over low heat. Serve once the desired texture is achieved. Garnish individual portions with chopped fresh herbs.

·· SOME FAVORITE AUTUMN VEGETABLES ··

carrot

· · · · · · · ·

butternut, kabocha or red kuri squash

· · · · · · · ·

daikon radish

· · · · · · · ·

parsnip

· · · · · · · ·

kohlrabi

· · · · · · · ·

white or sweet potato

· · · · · · · ·

turnip

· · · · · · · ·

MAINS

MAKES
4 boats

PREP TIME
5 minutes

COOK TIME
45 minutes

TOTAL TIME
50 minutes

BAKED ZUCCHINI BOATS

This easy dinner option is perfect for home veggie gardeners who end up with surplus zucchini on their hands during the heart of summer. Feel free to get creative with the filling and use different grains, nuts and dried fruits.

⅔ cup red quinoa, rinsed

⅔ cup water

1 Tablespoon coconut oil, or other oil of your choice

¼ teaspoon cinnamon

¼ cup hazelnuts, chopped

2 Tablespoons chopped dried cranberries

Dash of cayenne pepper (optional)

¼ teaspoon salt

2 large zucchini

Pesto for serving (see p. 192)

Bring water to a boil in a small saucepan. Add quinoa and reduce heat to low, then cover and cook for 20 minutes, or until all water is absorbed. When cooking is complete, remove from heat and keep covered.

While quinoa cooks, heat oil in a small skillet over medium heat. Add cinnamon, and stir for 30 seconds before adding hazelnuts. Cook for 5–7 minutes, until nuts are lightly toasted, stirring occasionally. Remove skillet from heat.

Once quinoa is cooked, preheat oven to 375 degrees. Add hazelnut mixture, cranberries, cayenne (if using) and salt to quinoa, and stir well. Taste and adjust seasoning as needed. Set quinoa aside while zucchini is prepared.

Remove stem ends of zucchini and cut each one in half lengthwise as evenly as possible. Using a small spoon, scoop out seeds, leaving outer flesh and skin intact. Place zucchini boats on a baking sheet.

Spoon the quinoa mixture neatly into each zucchini boat. Place in oven and bake for 18–25 minutes, until zucchini skins are bright green and can be easily pierced with a fork.

Serve immediately, accompanied by pesto. (I like to pipe a ribbon of pesto on top of each boat using a pastry bag.)

MAINS

SERVES
6

PREP TIME
15 minutes

COOK TIME
15 minutes

TOTAL TIME
30 minutes

CREAMY DIJON TEMPEH

I don't cook (or eat) much processed soy, but when I do, tempeh is my go-to choice. I love its dense texture and slightly nutty flavor. This easy skillet meal is great for weeknight dinners.

4 Tablespoons olive oil, divided

One 8-ounce package tempeh, cut into cubes (choose a gluten-free brand if needed)

1 small yellow onion, sliced into half-moons

½ pound cremini mushrooms, sliced

1 cup dry white wine

2 Tablespoons smooth Dijon mustard

½ teaspoon dried thyme

½ teaspoon dried tarragon

¼ cup raw cashews, soaked for at least 2 hours and drained

⅓ cup water

Salt and pepper

In a large skillet, heat 2 tablespoons of olive oil over medium heat. Add tempeh and fry, flipping as needed, until all sides are lightly browned. Transfer tempeh to a plate and set aside.

Add the remaining 2 tablespoons of oil to the same skillet, and sauté onions over medium heat for 2-3 minutes or until they begin to soften. Add mushrooms, season lightly with salt and pepper, and cook for 4-5 minutes or until mushrooms are soft and glistening.

Add the wine and raise heat to medium-high. When wine boils, reduce heat to low and stir in the mustard, thyme and tarragon. Simmer for 5 minutes.

While sauce cooks, place the drained cashews and water in a blender. Blend for 60-90 seconds or until very smooth (you may need to scrape down the sides of the blender a few times with a rubber spatula to get a super smooth consistency).

Add tempeh, cashew sauce and ½ teaspoon of salt to the sauce and stir well. Cook for another 5 minutes and then serve over a grain of your choice (I like to use red quinoa).

NOT YOUR MOTHER'S PLATE

As I prepared to write this book, I struggled with the idea of including a "Main Dishes" chapter. In many ways, thinking that a meal has to be a main dish plus accompanying side dishes seems like a bit of an antiquated idea, although the majority of readers of this book probably grew up with meals that followed this formula.

In my own meals at home, I am more likely to combine small portions of a few dishes we might commonly think of as side dishes to create a full meal. So please do not feel constrained in your cooking to make a meal resemble what you mother might have served you growing up.

I offer the dishes in this chapter as examples of heartier dishes, many of which can stand as a meal on their own. When you are cooking for family members or friends who are accustomed to more of a standard American diet and might be intimidated by the notion of a meat-free meal, I suggest you take a recipe from this chapter to show your guests just how nourishing the experience can be.

Likewise, I encourage you to create your own meals combining various recipes from other chapters of this book to your heart's delight. People are often funny when it comes to creating menus and struggle with the notion that they have to get it right somehow. If you are feeling intimidated by creating a menu yourself, I suggest focusing on including dishes that are different colors, flavors, textures, and temperatures. Not only is it fun to have variety, but psychologically, the brain registers a greater sense of satiation when our meals are varied.

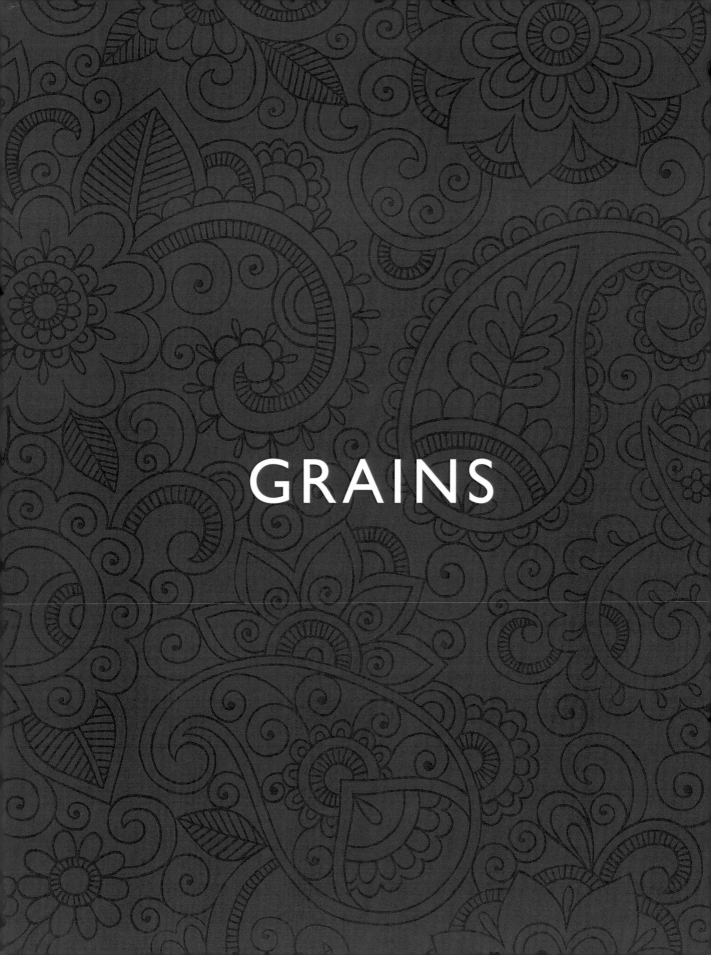

GRAINS

ROSEMARY GARLIC POLENTA

MILLET WITH SWEET POTATO & OLIVES

BLACK RICE & ROASTED PINEAPPLE SALAD

QUINOA WITH CURRANTS & ALMONDS

QUINOA TABBOULEH

TOASTED FARRO WITH ROASTED VEGETABLES

BASMATI RICE PILAU

GRAINS

SERVES
6

PREP TIME
5 minutes

COOK TIME
40 minutes

TOTAL TIME
45 minutes

ROSEMARY GARLIC POLENTA

One of my favorite simple meals is this polenta with black beans and sautéed greens. Polenta can be made with any type of cornmeal, not only coarse versions specifically labeled as polenta.

4 cups water

1 Tablespoon ghee (use vegan butter for a vegan option)

2 cloves garlic, minced

2 teaspoons chopped fresh rosemary

1 teaspoon salt

1 cup polenta/cornmeal

Add all ingredients except polenta to a heavy-bottomed medium pot and bring to a boil over high heat. Slowly pour polenta into the pot while whisking continuously. Turn heat to low and continue to whisk until mixture has thickened slightly.

Continue cooking polenta for 30–40 minutes until it is very thick and the grains are fully cooked. Stir polenta every 8–10 minutes with a wooden spoon to keep it from sticking to the bottom of the pot. You may add additional water while cooking if polenta becomes too thick. Taste polenta once fully cooked and adjust salt as desired. Serve immediately.

MILLET WITH SWEET POTATO & OLIVES

SERVES 6

PREP TIME 10 minutes

COOK TIME 1 hour

TOTAL TIME 1 hour 10 minutes

Millet often gets a bad rap as a "boring" grain because of its subtle flavor. The key to preparing millet well is to lightly toast it before cooking. This warm salad is one of my favorite ways to enjoy millet.

1 large sweet potato, diced into ½-inch cubes

1 teaspoon olive oil

1 cup millet

2 cups water

½ cup pitted kalamata olives, halved

Zest and juice of 1 orange

½ teaspoon chopped fresh thyme, plus sprigs for garnish

Salt

Preheat oven to 375 degrees.

Toss sweet potato and olive oil together in a bowl and lightly season with salt. Place sweet potato in a single layer on a baking sheet and roast for 20–25 minutes or until tender, flipping once halfway through. Set aside to cool slightly.

While sweet potato roasts, dry-toast millet in a medium heavy-bottomed saucepan over medium heat for 4–6 minutes or until millet is slightly golden and fragrant. Stir millet often so that it does not burn.

Carefully add the water to the pan (it may sputter a bit), along with a couple of pinches of salt. Raise heat to high and bring millet to a boil, then cover pot and reduce heat to low. Cook millet for 20–25 minutes, or until all water has been absorbed. Remove millet from heat and let it steam for an additional 5–10 minutes away from heat.

Use a fork to gently fluff the millet as you transfer it to a medium mixing bowl. Add sweet potato, olives, orange zest and juice, thyme and ½ teaspoon salt and gently mix everything together. Adjust seasonings as desired and then serve immediately, garnished with fresh thyme sprigs.

GRAINS

SERVES
6

PREP TIME
15 minutes

COOK TIME
35 minutes

TOTAL TIME
50 minutes

BLACK RICE & ROASTED PINEAPPLE SALAD

Black rice is one of my favorite ingredients to use because of its beautiful purple hue once cooked. Roasting the pineapple diminishes its sourness and brings out more of its sweet flavor.

1½ cups black forbidden rice

1 small pineapple

¼ cup chopped basil, plus extra for garnish

¼ cup chopped Italian parsley, plus extra for garnish

⅓ cup walnuts, lightly toasted

2 Tablespoons olive oil

Salt and pepper

Preheat oven to 375 degrees.

Bring 2⅔ cups water to a boil in a medium pot, then add rice. Cover pot, reduce heat to low, and cook for 30–35 minutes or until all water is absorbed.

While rice cooks, quarter the pineapple lengthwise and remove the core. Place the pineapple skin-side down on a baking tray and bake for 20 minutes. Remove and let the pineapple cool. Use a knife to cut the skin off the pineapple before cutting it into small (½-inch) cubes.

Once the rice is cooked, place it in a medium-sized mixing bowl and let it cool to room temperature. Once cool, add cubed pineapple, herbs, walnuts and olive oil. Stir well, and season with salt and pepper to taste. Transfer to a serving bowl and top with chopped basil and parsley, or refrigerate until ready to serve.

GRAINS

SERVES
4

PREP TIME
10 minutes

COOK TIME
20 minutes

TOTAL TIME
30 minutes

QUINOA WITH CURRANTS AND ALMONDS

This simple side dish is a great accompaniment to my Autumn Vegetable Tagine (p. 90) or any hearty stew. You can of course substitute any combination of dried fruits and nuts that you like, but this is my go-to pairing.

2 cups water

1 cup white quinoa, rinsed

¼ cup slivered almonds

¼ cup dried currants

Preheat oven or toaster oven to 350 degrees.

In a small pot, bring water to a boil over high heat. Add quinoa and cover pot. Reduce heat to low and cook for 20 minutes, or until all water has been absorbed. Turn off flame and let quinoa steam for an additional 5 minutes.

While the quinoa cooks, spread the almonds on a small baking sheet and cook in the preheated oven for 4–6 minutes, or until lightly brown and fragrant. Remove from oven and set aside.

Once the quinoa has steamed, gently fold in the toasted almonds and currants. Keep covered until ready to serve.

QUINOA TABBOULEH

SERVES 6

PREP TIME 20 minutes

TOTAL TIME 20 minutes

I've gotten into the habit of making my tabbouleh with quinoa in place of bulgur wheat since many of the retreats I cater require gluten-free options. I like using different colored heirloom tomatoes to enhance the tabbouleh's appearance. You can also substitute multicolored grape or cherry tomatoes in place of the heirlooms.

- 3 cups cooked and chilled quinoa
- 2 large heirloom tomatoes, diced
- 2 Persian cucumbers, diced
- 1 cup chopped parsley (plus additional for garnish)
- ¼ cup chopped fresh mint (plus additional for garnish)
- ½ cup lemon juice
- ¼ cup olive oil
- ¾ teaspoon salt

Place quinoa, tomato, cucumber and fresh herbs in a large mixing bowl and mix together gently using a spatula.

Whisk together all remaining ingredients in a small bowl. Add to quinoa and mix well. Taste and add more lemon juice and/or salt as desired. Garnish with fresh herbs and serve immediately or cover and refrigerate (I recommend the latter—tabbouleh is generally best a few hours after it was prepared.)

GRAINS

TOASTED FARRO SALAD WITH ROASTED VEGETABLES

V

SERVES 6

PREP TIME 30 minutes

COOK TIME 20 minutes

TOTAL TIME 50 minutes + cooling

A friend from Italy turned me on to how wonderful farro salads are during the summer. I created this salad to use peak summertime produce, but it can be adapted by roasting whatever vegetables happen to be in season.

1 small eggplant, cut into ½-inch slices

2 zucchinis, quartered lengthwise and chopped

2 yellow squash, quartered lengthwise and chopped

1 small red onion, chopped

1 red bell pepper, chopped

2 Tablespoons olive oil, divided

Salt and pepper

1½ cups farro (whole-grain, not pearled)

1 teaspoon each: chopped fresh mint, basil and oregano

2 Tablespoons lemon juice

Pre-heat oven to 375 degrees. Rub the sides of each eggplant round lightly with salt and place in a small bowl for 10–15 minutes. Wipe any excess liquid off the eggplant and cut each slice into cubes. Toss the eggplant, squash, onion and red bell pepper with 1 tablespoon of olive oil and place in a single layer on a larger baking sheet. Season vegetables lightly with salt and pepper. Roast for 16-20 minutes or until tender, flipping vegetables halfway during cooking. Remove from oven and let them cool fully.

While vegetables cook, bring a medium pot of salted water to a boil. While you wait for the water to boil, dry-toast farro in a medium skillet over a medium flame, stirring often until farro becomes slightly fragrant (about 4–6 minutes). When water boils, add toasted farro to the pot and cook for 12–15 minutes or until farro is your desired al dente texture. Drain farro well and then transfer to a large bowl and let it cool to lukewarm temperature.

Once both the farro and vegetables are cool, add the vegetables to the large bowl along with all the remaining ingredients. Stir well, seasoning with salt and pepper to taste. Allow the salad to sit for at least 20 minutes prior to serving.

GRAINS

SERVES
4

PREP TIME
5 minutes

COOK TIME
20 minutes

TOTAL TIME
25 minutes

BASMATI RICE PILAU

Pilau (from the same root as "pilaf") is a traditional rice dish common in Indian cooking, and can be sweet or savory in flavor. In Ayurveda, white basmati rice is favored because it is more easily digested. If you use a variety that was grown in India, it also has a flavor that is unparalleled. The cooking method for the rice used here is inspired by Persian cooking and helps to ensure a perfect texture.

2 cups water

1 cup white Indian basmati rice, rinsed

¼ cup shelled pistachios (unsalted)

⅛ cup golden raisins

Pre-heat oven or toaster oven to 350 degrees.

Heat water in a medium pot with a tight-fitting lid over high heat. While you wait for the water to boil, prepare the lid for the pot by wrapping it in a tea towel. When boiling, add rice and cover the pot with the towel-wrapped lid. Turn heat to low and cook for 20 minutes or until all water is absorbed.

While rice cooks, spread the pistachios on a small baking sheet and cook in the preheated oven for 4-6 minutes, or until lightly brown and fragrant. Remove from oven and set aside.

When rice has finished cooking, turn off heat, add raisins and let it steam for 5 minutes, covered. After steaming is complete, add toasted pistachios and use a large fork to fluff rice and fold in raisins and nuts. Keep covered until ready to serve.

THE CASE FOR ORGANIC FOOD

Each time we cook, we have the opportunity to make compassionate choices, and for me, choosing organic ingredients is about kindness. The way I see it, the decision to choose organic is not only about the health of myself and my friends and families but very much about the health of agricultural workers and employees in pesticide factories who can suffer great consequences from repeated exposure to harsh chemical compounds.

I also see buying organic food as a way of being kind to the Earth. Thousands of gallons of inorganic pesticide, herbicide, and fertilizer runoff ends up in waterways each year, polluting drinking water supplies and recreational areas and devastating aquatic life.

If you're on a budget and can't afford to go 100% organic, check out the Dirty Dozen list that is put out and updated annually by the Environmental Working Group (http://ewg.org). It identifies the produce with the highest amounts of pesticide residues and recommends always buying these 12 foods from organic producers only. On the flipside, the EWG also publishes a yearly Clean 15 list with foods that are generally produced without any chemicals (or only very small trace amounts).

When you shop at a local farmers market, look for organic signs to guide you but also get to know the farmers and their growing methods. Many small family farms do not seek out organic certification, which can cost them upward of $25,000 annually. Ask farmers what sprays and pesticides they use and do some research to learn about them. Look for farms that grow different types of seasonal produce throughout the year because, in my experience, they tend to be more in sync with natural growing practices.

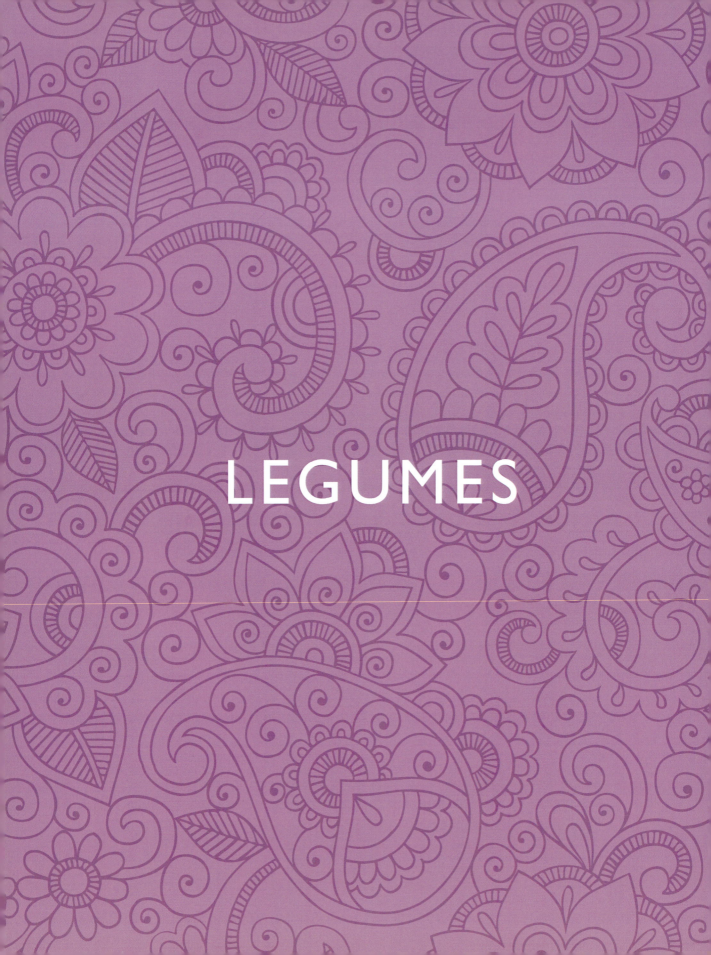

LEGUMES

BASIC BEANS

GREEN CHILE STEW

WHITE BEAN RAGOUT
WITH SUNDRIED TOMATOES

MUNG DAL TADKA

RED LENTIL DAL WITH TAMARIND

COCONUT CURRY DAL

BLACK BEAN & EDAMAME SALAD

FRENCH GREEN LENTIL SALAD

LEGUMES

SERVES
6

PREP TIME
5 minutes

COOK TIME
1 hour
30 minutes

TOTAL TIME
1 hour
35 minutes
+ soaking

BASIC BEANS

This is my go-to preparation for simple beans that can be paired with just about anything to make a meal.

1 cup dried beans, soaked overnight and drained

1 bay leaf

1 pinch hing (optional)

1 teaspoon ghee (or oil of your choice for a vegan option)

1 small onion, finely diced

1 teaspoon ground cumin

1½ teaspoons salt

Place drained beans in a medium pot and cover with water by about an inch. Bring to a boil and skim off any foam. Add bay leaf and hing (if using) and cover the pot. Reduce heat to low and simmer beans for 1–1½ hours or until desired texture is achieved.

While beans are cooking, heat ghee/oil in a small skillet over medium-high heat and sauté onion for 5-6 minutes or until translucent. Stir in cumin and sauté for 1 minute longer. Remove skillet from heat and set aside.

When beans are cooked, add onion mixture along with salt. Stir well and cook for an additional 5-10 minutes.

Optional: For a creamier consistency, use a ladle to scoop out about 1 cup of beans. Transfer to a small bowl and mash well with a fork. Stir mashed beans back into the pot. Taste and adjust seasonings before serving.

LEGUMES

GREEN CHILE STEW

SERVES
4

My father lives in New Mexico where the state's famed crop (and source of much pride) is the Hatch green chile. He ships me boxes of chiles each year, and this stew is one of my favorite uses for them. Feel free to use any combination of beans you wish.

PREP TIME
20 minutes

COOK TIME
30 minutes

TOTAL TIME
1 hour

1 Tablespoon olive oil

1 onion, diced

2 carrots, diced

2 celery stalks, diced

¼ pound tomatillos, chopped

2 cloves garlic, minced

1 teaspoon ground cumin

1 teaspoon chile powder

¼ teaspoon dried oregano

1–2 frozen Hatch green chiles, chopped*

1½ cups cooked black beans**

1 cup cooked black-eyed peas**

2½ cups vegetable broth

1 teaspoon salt

Lime wedges and chopped cilantro for serving

HATCH CHILES are available fresh for a small window in late summer, but can otherwise be purchased frozen online. Be sure to use roasted and peeled chiles for this recipe. Remove seeds and inner ribs before chopping if you prefer less heat.

Canned green chile may be used if necessary.

** As a general guideline, beans roughly triple in volume when cooked, so measure out dried beans accordingly if you plan to start from scratch.

Heat oil in a large saucepan or small stockpot over medium heat. Add onion, carrot and celery and sauté until vegetables begin to soften, about 5-6 minutes. Add in tomatillos and cook an additional 5 minutes, stirring often, until they are soft and beginning to lose their shape. Add garlic and sauté for about 1 minute more, until it is fragrant. Stir in dry spices and chiles.

Add beans, black-eyed peas and vegetable broth, and bring to a boil. Then reduce heat, cover pot and simmer the stew for 20-25 minutes. Stir in salt and cook a few minutes more, then adjust seasonings as desired. Serve in individual bowls garnished with lime wedges and a sprinkle of cilantro.

WHITE BEAN RAGOUT WITH SUNDRIED TOMATOES

SERVES
4–6

PREP TIME
15 minutes

COOK TIME
1 hour
10 minutes

TOTAL TIME
1 hour
25 minutes

This is a vegan spin on a French classic. Umami-rich sundried tomatoes stand in for pork and add color in addition to flavor.

1 cup Great Northern or navy beans, soaked overnight and drained

½ cup sundried tomatoes (not oil-packed)

2 teaspoons olive oil

1 onion, diced

2 cloves garlic, minced

1 teaspoon fresh thyme, chopped

¾ teaspoon salt

Place sundried tomatoes in a small bowl and cover with boiling water. Drain after 5 minutes and rinse tomatoes with cool water. Chop tomatoes into small pieces and set aside.

Place drained beans in a medium pot and add enough water to just cover the top of the beans. Bring to a boil and skim off any foam. Cook for about an hour or until beans are tender, stirring occasionally. (Add more water if beans become too dry while cooking but avoid having too much liquid.)

While beans cook, heat oil in a medium skillet and add onion. Cook for 15–20 minutes over low heat until onion is slightly caramelized. Stir in sundried tomatoes, garlic and thyme, and cook for an additional 5 minutes. Set skillet aside.

When beans are tender, stir in the onion mixture and salt and cook for 10 minutes. Taste and adjust salt before serving.

LEGUMES

SERVES
4

PREP TIME
5 minutes

COOK TIME
40 minutes

TOTAL TIME
45 minutes

MUNG DAL TADKA

This dal is commonly found in Indian restaurants, often as an appetizer soup. It's great it on its own or as part of a larger feast. I especially love it on winter nights when plans require me to eat a bit later than usual and I want to keep things on the lighter side.

1 cup split yellow mung beans, soaked for 2–3 hours and drained

1 tomato, diced

¼ teaspoon turmeric powder

3½ cups water

1 serrano chile, halved and seeds removed (optional)

1 Tablespoon ghee (or coconut oil for vegan option)

1 teaspoon cumin seeds

¾ teaspoon brown mustard seeds

1 Tablespoon fresh grated ginger

1 pinch hing (optional)

½ teaspoon salt

Place mung beans, tomato, turmeric, water and chile (if using) in a medium pot and bring to a boil over high heat. Skim off any foam and lower heat to a simmer. Cook covered for 20-30 minutes, or until beans are very soft.

While beans cook, heat the ghee/oil in a small skillet over a medium-low flame. Add cumin, mustard seeds, ginger and hing and stir often. Once mustard seeds begin to pop, remove the skillet from the stove.

Add sautéed spices to the mung beans once they are soft and cook for 5-10 minutes to let flavors settle. Add salt and adjust to taste. Serve dal over basmati rice or in bowls on its own.

LEGUMES

SERVES
4

PREP TIME
10 minutes

COOK TIME
40 minutes

TOTAL TIME
50 minutes

RED LENTIL DAL WITH TAMARIND

A magazine recipe I stumbled upon years ago inspired this recipe and it has since become a staple on retreats I cook for. The unique sour flavor of tamarind gives this dal a flavor that is out of this world. You can find tamarind paste at Indian markets and at many more mainstream groceries as well.

1 cup red lentils, rinsed

¼ teaspoon turmeric powder

2 Tablespoons ghee (or sunflower oil for a vegan option)

½ teaspoon each: yellow mustard seeds, fennel seeds, ground coriander

1 serrano chile, halved and seeds removed

1 large red onion, thinly sliced into half-moons

1 teaspoon tamarind paste

¾ teaspoon salt

Place lentils and 3-4 cups water (use more for a soupier dal) in a medium heavy-bottomed pot and bring to a boil over high heat. Skim off any foam and stir in the turmeric. Cover pot partially and simmer over fairly low heat, stirring occasionally, until the lentils begin to break down (about 15-20 minutes).

While lentils cook, heat the oil in a medium skillet over medium heat. Add the mustard seeds and cook until they start to pop. Add the fennel seeds, coriander and chile and stir until fragrant (about 30 seconds). Stir in the onion and cook over low heat for 15-20 minutes or until onions are very soft and slightly caramelized. Stir skillet mixture occasionally to prevent burning.

Once the onion and spice mixture is ready, stir it into the cooked lentils. Whisk the tamarind paste together with ¼ cup hot water and then stir it into the lentils. Cook dal for at least 15-20 minutes longer over a low flame. Season the dal with salt and adjust before serving. Serve over rice (it goes especially well with the basmati pilau on p. 106) or as a soup for a first course.

COCONUT CURRY DAL

SERVES
4

PREP TIME
10 minutes

COOK TIME
40 minutes

TOTAL TIME
50 minutes

I often hear that Indian cooking is intimidating because recipes can call for well over a dozen spices. In this creamy dal, I use common spice blends to reduce the number of spices you need to purchase.

1 cup red lentils, rinsed

3 Tablespoons ghee (or coconut oil for a vegan option), divided

1 small onion, minced

2 cloves garlic, minced

1½ teaspoons garam masala

¾ teaspoon curry powder

½ teaspoon turmeric powder

1 pinch hing (optional)

1 cup full-fat coconut milk

¾ teaspoon salt

2 shallots, diced

¼ teaspoon red pepper flakes

2 bay leaves

1 teaspoon brown mustard seeds

Chopped cilantro for serving

In a medium heavy-bottomed pot, melt 2 tablespoons of ghee/oil over medium-high heat and then sauté onion and garlic for 2–3 minutes. Add lentils, garam masala, curry powder, turmeric, hing (if using) and 3 cups of water. Bring to a boil and skim off any foam. Cover pot partially and simmer over fairly low heat, stirring occasionally, until the lentils begin to break down (about 15–20 minutes). Add coconut milk and salt to lentils and cook for an additional 10 minutes.

To finish the dal, heat the remaining 1 tablespoon of ghee/oil over high heat. Add the shallot, red pepper, bay leaves and mustard seeds, and sauté about 1 minute or until mustard seeds begin to pop. Stir spice mixture into lentils and cook for 5 minutes. Taste and adjust salt as needed. Serve dal over rice or on its own, garnished with cilantro.

LEGUMES

SERVES
4

PREP TIME
10 minutes

COOK TIME
5 minutes

TOTAL TIME
15 minutes

BLACK BEAN & EDAMAME SALAD

This quick salad can be whipped up in minutes as part of a weeknight dinner. I call for using canned beans, but you can, of course, cook your own instead. You can also add shredded carrot, sliced snap peas or other vegetables to add color and variety to the basic recipe.

1 cup frozen shelled edamame

1 can black beans, drained and rinsed

2 scallions (greens and whites), thinly sliced

2 teaspoons grapeseed oil

1 teaspoon sesame oil

1 teaspoon apple cider vinegar

1 teaspoon honey (or maple syrup for a vegan option)

1 teaspoon grated fresh ginger

¼ teaspoon salt

1 Tablespoon toasted sesame seeds for garnish (optional)

Bring a small pot of water to a boil. Add edamame and cook for 2 minutes. Drain and rinse with cold water. While edamame cools, whisk together oils, vinegar, honey/maple syrup, ginger and salt in a small bowl.

Combine drained edamame with black beans and scallion in a large bowl. Add dressing and toss to coat beans. Sprinkle sesame seeds over salad (if using). Serve salad immediately or refrigerate until ready to eat.

FRENCH GREEN LENTIL SALAD

SERVES 6

PREP TIME
10 minutes

COOK TIME
20 minutes

TOTAL TIME
30 minutes
+ chilling

Fennel, olives and lentils are a match made in heaven. Try this salad and experience the perfect trifecta for yourself.

1 cup French green lentils, rinsed

1 bulb fennel, thinly sliced

¼ cup + ½ teaspoon olive oil, divided

½ cup pitted Kalamata olives, halved

1 Tablespoon white wine vinegar

1 teaspoon smooth Dijon mustard

¼ teaspoon dried thyme

Salt and pepper

Preheat oven to 375 degrees.

Place lentils in a medium saucepan and add enough water to cover by 1 inch. Bring lentils to a boil, then cover and cook for 15-17 minutes, or until lentils are tender but not mushy. Drain lentils and rinse with cool water. Place rinsed lentils in a medium mixing bowl to cool.

While lentils cook, toss the sliced fennel with ½ teaspoon olive oil. Place fennel on a baking sheet in an even layer and lightly season with salt and pepper. Roast fennel for 15-20 minutes or until edges are lightly browned, flipping once halfway through cooking.

Add the roasted fennel and olives to the mixing bowl with the lentils. Prepare dressing by whisking together ¼ cup olive oil with the vinegar, mustard, thyme and ¼ teaspoon salt in a small bowl. Pour dressing over salad and stir well. Refrigerate salad for at least an hour to let the flavors meld, letting it come to room temperature before serving.

SALADS

BEET, KALE & POMEGRANATE SALAD

WINTER KALE SALAD

CORN, TOMATO & AVOCADO SALAD

ARUGULA & RADISH SALAD

FALL HARVEST SALAD

SPRINGTIME SALAD WITH KUMQUATS

ORANGE, OLIVE & FENNEL SALAD

TAHINI KALE SALAD

SALADS

SERVES
6

PREP TIME
20 minutes

TOTAL TIME
20 minutes
+ marinating time

BEET, KALE & POMEGRANATE SALAD

This is one of my most-requested recipes at the retreats I cook for. If pomegranate is not in season, you can omit it or use dried cranberries in its place.

¼ cup balsamic vinegar

2 Tablespoons Dijon mustard

1 teaspoon salt

¼ cup olive oil

1 bunch curly green kale, de-ribbed and cut into thin ribbons

¼ cup walnuts, coarsely chopped

2 pounds red beets, peeled and grated

½ cup pomegranate arils*, plus extra for serving

Whisk together vinegar, mustard and salt in a small bowl. Slowly drizzle in olive oil, whisking constantly until dressing is emulsified.

Place prepared kale in a large bowl and pour dressing over it. Use your hands to massage the dressing into the kale until it becomes noticeably softer. Let the kale marinate for 20–30 minutes.

While the kale marinates, toast walnuts in a preheated 350-degree oven for 4–5 minutes, or until fragrant and slightly darker. Remove from oven and set aside to cool.

Add beets, pomegranate arils and toasted walnuts to the kale and stir well. Top the salad with extra pomegranate arils and serve. This salad can also be made ahead of time and refrigerated but should be brought closer to room temperature before serving.

*Commonly called seeds

SALADS

WINTER KALE SALAD

SERVES
4

PREP TIME
15 minutes

TOTAL TIME
15 minutes
+ marinating time

I developed this salad years ago for a client to serve at her family's Christmas gathering and it's now become a staple for me during the winter months.

1 large bunch lacinato kale, de-ribbed and cut into bite-sized pieces

3 Tablespoons olive oil

1 Tablespoon lemon juice

1/2 teaspoon ground cumin

1 Asian pear, diced

4 leaves of radicchio, cut into thin ribbons

1 small bulb of fennel, halved lengthwise and thinly sliced

2 Tablespoons pumpkin seeds, plus extra for serving

Salt and pepper

Place the prepared kale in a large bowl.

Combine olive oil, lemon juice, cumin and a couple pinches of salt in a small jar and shake until emulsified. Pour this dressing over the kale and massage lightly using your hands until kale begins to soften slightly. Let kale marinate for 20–30 minutes.

Add the pear, radicchio, fennel and pumpkin seeds, and toss well. Season salad with salt and pepper to taste. Garnish with additional pumpkin seeds and serve. This salad can be made ahead of time and refrigerated but should be brought closer to room temperature before serving.

SALADS

CORN, TOMATO & AVOCADO SALAD

SERVES
4

PREP TIME
15 minutes

TOTAL TIME
15 minutes

Meet your new go-to summertime salad. Be sure to use the freshest ingredients you can find for the best results.

4 large ears of corn, shucked

1 cup grape or cherry tomatoes, halved

1 large avocado, diced

1 large handful cilantro, chopped*

1 Tablespoon olive oil

Juice of 1 lime

¼ teaspoon salt

Use a knife to remove the kernels from each ear of corn, cutting very close to the cob. Place corn kernels in a medium bowl and add all remaining ingredients. Stir well and serve immediately. If you choose to make this salad in advance, be sure to slice and add the avocado just before serving.

* Thinly-sliced basil can be substituted for cilantro.

SALADS

SERVES
4

PREP TIME
10 minutes

TOTAL TIME
10 minutes

SPRINGTIME SALAD WITH KUMQUATS

When you are lucky enough to have kumquats in season, you should put them in everything, including your salads. Use a paring knife to thinly slice them and remove any seeds before using for the best visual effect.

2–3 heads Little Gems or other baby lettuce

1 small Persian cucumber, sliced

10 sugar snap peas, thinly sliced

6 kumquats, thinly sliced

Preserved Lemon Vinaigrette (see p. 200)

Separate lettuce leaves and arrange them across four salad plates. Sprinkle one quarter of the cucumber, snap peas and kumquat slices over each salad. Serve immediately with dressing on the side and let everyone dress their salad to their liking.

SALADS

SERVES
4

PREP TIME
10 minutes

TOTAL TIME
10 minutes

FALL HARVEST SALAD

The sweet flavors of this salad help to balance the energy of the fall, when many of us feel a bit scattered and ungrounded. You can also add roasted root vegetables to this recipe for even more grounding.

⅓ pound baby salad greens

1 apple, thinly sliced

1 pear, thinly sliced

1 persimmon, thinly sliced

2 Tablespoons golden raisins

1 batch Persimmon Vinaigrette (see p. 201)

2 Tablespoons pecans

Divide greens between 4 salad plates. Arrange the fruits over each portion of greens. Just before serving, drizzle a spoonful of vinaigrette over each salad. Top each salad with pecans and serve immediately.

For a family style meal, you can toss all ingredients together in a large bowl and serve the dressing on the side.

ARUGULA & RADISH SALAD

SERVES
4

PREP TIME
10 minutes

TOTAL TIME
10 minutes

I absolutely love the pungent combination of the two stars of this salad. The sourness of the dressing adds an additional depth of flavor.

1 Tablespoon pumpkin seeds

1 Tablespoon sunflower seeds

⅓ pound wild arugula

⅓ cup sliced radishes

¼ cup Lemon Hempseed Dressing (see p. 202)

Heat a small skillet over medium flame. When hot, add pumpkin and sunflower seeds and toast, stirring often, for 2–3 minutes or until seeds become fragrant. Let seeds cool away from heat.

Once seeds are cool, toss them together with the arugula and radishes in a large bowl. Serve salad with the dressing on the side for a family-style meal, or lightly toss salad with a few spoonfuls of dressing and plate individual portions.

SALADS

SERVES
4

PREP TIME
15 minutes

TOTAL TIME
15 minutes

ORANGE, OLIVE & FENNEL SALAD

As you may notice, I am quite a minimalist when it comes to salads. I love selecting a few quality ingredients that speak for themselves. This salad was developed in Fes, Morocco, using the best ingredients in the market on that particular spring day.

3 large oranges

1 large fennel bulb, halved lengthwise and sliced very thinly

1 teaspoon orange juice

1 teaspoon good quality olive oil

¾ cup oil-cured olives, drained

Salt and pepper

Fennel fronds for serving

Prepare each orange by slicing off tops and bottoms of the rind. Set one of the cut ends down on your cutting board, then use a knife to carefully cut the rind and white pith from the flesh of the orange. As you work, follow the natural curves of the fruit. Once all oranges are peeled, thinly slice each orange into rounds, then divide the rounds between 4 salad plates.

In a small bowl, whisk together orange juice and olive oil and season lightly with salt and pepper. Add the fennel and gently toss to coat it with dressing. Place one quarter of the dressed fennel and olives over each portion of orange slices. Garnish each salad with a sprinkle of fennel fronds and serve.

SALADS

SERVES
4

PREP TIME
10 minutes

TOTAL TIME
10 minutes
+ marinating

TAHINI KALE SALAD

When I was still working a corporate job, this was often my default lunch salad. It is best when eaten the same day it is made.

1 large bunch curly green kale, de-ribbed and torn into bite-sized pieces

1 Tablespoon lemon juice

¾ teaspoon salt

2 Tablespoons tahini

1 teaspoon soy sauce (use tamari for a gluten-free option)

1 small carrot, grated or thinly julienned

Black sesame seeds for serving

Place kale in a large bowl. Sprinkle lemon juice and salt over the kale, and then use your hands to massage the dressing into the kale until it becomes noticeably softer. Let the kale marinate for 20-30 minutes.

In a small bowl, whisk together the tahini and soy sauce (it will become thick like a paste). Transfer the tahini mixture to the kale, and use your hands to rub the two together. Keep rubbing until the kale is evenly coated with tahini.

Gently fold the carrot into the salad. Transfer salad to a serving bowl and garnish with black sesame seeds before serving.

IT'S NOT JUST WHAT YOU EAT

We have all been told that we are what we eat, and while our food choices do matter, there is far more to the picture. I tell my clients that it's not just what you eat, it's what you absorb and assimilate that determines how much nutrition you actually receive from the food you consume.

One of the ways food becomes more digestible is through the process of cooking. When food is heated, cell walls become more malleable and may begin to break down, easing the work that the body's digestive enzymes have to do once the food reaches the digestive organs. The steps we take prior to heating food (like soaking beans, for example) can also affect its digestive outcomes.

Likewise, massaging raw foods, especially hearty greens like kale, helps to soften cell walls and aid in digestion. One of my biggest pet peeves when I eat out is ordering kale salads only to find that the kale has not been massaged. I rarely feel good after eating unmassaged raw kale, and the taste is far less pleasant as well. I have now learned to ask my server about this before ordering.

To massage kale, simply grab handfuls at a time and use your fingers to rub it around your palms. If you have children, this is a great task to assign to them. I have had numerous parents report that their children suddenly started eating their greens once they had the opportunity to get their hands on it.

You can further reap the benefits of good digestion by always taking the time to chew your food well. Some people like to recommend to chew a certain number of times before you swallow, but I would just encourage you to chew solid foods to the point where they become mostly liquid. On the flip side, resist the temptation to slurp down liquids like pureed soups and smoothies. Instead, let those linger a second so they can mix with your mouth's digestive enzymes to kick-start their digestive journey.

VEGGIE SIDES

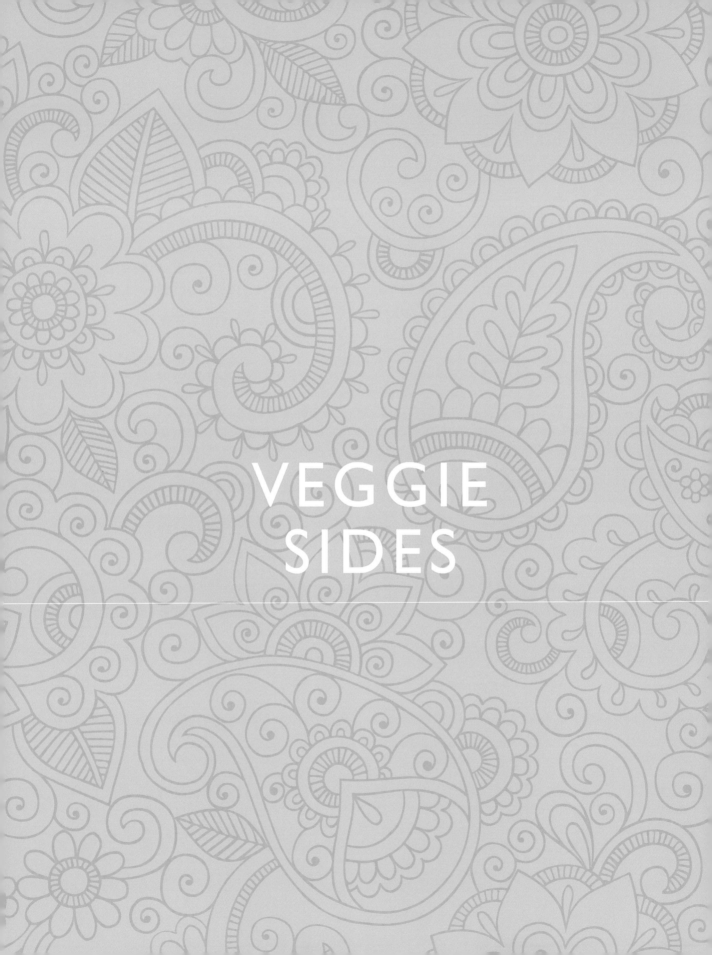

ZA'ATAR CARROTS

ZUCCHINI WITH HAZELNUT CRUMBLE

ROASTED CAULIFLOWER WITH CAPERS

SAUTÉED MIXED MUSHROOMS

SIMPLE GREENS

MAPLE-GINGER GLAZED ACORN SQUASH

TURMERIC SWEET POTATO HASH

MAPLE-BALSAMIC BRUSSELS SPROUTS

HORSERADISH MASHED POTATOES

SPICED OKRA WITH PEANUTS

ROASTED BROCCOLI WITH MEYER LEMON

STIR-FRIED SAVOY CABBAGE & SHIITAKES

CARROT, DAIKON & HIJIKI STIR-FRY

ROASTED EGGPLANT WITH CILANTRO

POTATO AND GREEN BEAN SUBJI

MOROCCAN CAULIFLOWER

DIJON DILL POTATOES

VEGGIE SIDES

SWEET ZA'ATAR CARROTS

SERVES
4

PREP TIME
5 minutes

COOK TIME
25 minutes

TOTAL TIME
30 minutes

Like so many of the best recipes, this one came about spontaneously using various items I had in my pantry. This basic preparation works well with winter squashes and other roasted vegetables as well.

1 pound carrots

1 Tablespoon olive oil

2 Tablespoons maple syrup

¾ teaspoon za'atar (see p. 215), plus extra for garnish

Salt

Preheat oven to 375 degrees.

While oven heats, wash and prepare carrots. For small, delicate farmers market carrots, I like to leave them whole and snip off the leaves just above the top of the carrot, allowing just a touch of green to remain. For larger carrots, chop into roughly ½-inch rounds or half-moons. Once carrots are prepared, toss them with the oil and a few pinches of salt, and then place on a baking sheet in a single layer. Bake for 20–25 minutes, or until carrots are just fork-tender, flipping once with a spatula about halfway through.

When carrots are finished cooking, let them cool for a couple minutes and then gently toss them with the maple syrup and za'atar. (I do this very carefully directly on the tray, but you could also use a large bowl for this purpose.) Place on a serving platter and sprinkle a few pinches of za'atar over the carrots. Serve immediately. Any leftovers are wonderful cold in salads or on their own the next day.

VEGGIE SIDES

SERVES
4–6

PREP TIME
15 minutes

COOK TIME
15 minutes

TOTAL TIME
30 minutes

ZUCCHINI WITH HAZELNUT CRUMBLE

Consider making extra hazelnut crumble and adding it to all your favorite things. Several moms I've shared this with have told me it is their secret way to get their kids to eat more veggies.

¼ cup hazelnuts, aka filberts

2 cloves garlic

2 teaspoons coconut oil

2 pounds zucchini, halved lengthwise and cut into half-moons

½ teaspoon dried marjoram (or 1 teaspoon chopped fresh leaves)

Salt

Preheat oven or toaster oven to 350 degrees.

Place hazelnuts on a rimmed baking sheet in a single layer and toast for 8–10 minutes, or until fragrant and slightly darker. Transfer nuts to the center of a clean dishtowel. Wrap the towel around the nuts and use your hands to slough the skins off the nuts (it's okay if some skin remains).

Place peeled nuts and garlic in a mini-food processor or blender. Pulse a few times until nuts are coarsely chopped and crumbly. Season mixture with a couple pinches of salt, pulse once more, and then set mixture aside.

Heat the oil in a large skillet over medium-high heat and add the zucchini and marjoram. Stir-fry for 4–5 minutes, or until zucchini is just fork-tender. Transfer zucchini to a shallow serving dish and sprinkle the hazelnut crumble over the top. Serve immediately.

ROASTED CAULIFLOWER WITH CAPERS

SERVES
4–6

PREP TIME
10 minutes

COOK TIME
20 minutes

TOTAL TIME
30 minutes

I grew up eating boiled cauliflower and never developed an appreciation for it until I learned to roast it. Now, cauliflower is one of my favorite things to cook. This easy preparation is always a hit.

1 large head cauliflower, chopped into medium florets

1 Tablespoon olive oil

Aleppo or other crushed red pepper flakes

2 Tablespoons capers, drained

1 Tablespoon red wine vinegar

Salt

Chopped parsley for serving

Preheat oven to 425 degrees.

Toss the cauliflower and olive oil together in a medium bowl and season lightly with salt. Spread the prepared cauliflower on a large baking sheet in a single layer. Bake for 10–12 minutes, or until char marks are present, and then turn florets using a spatula. Cook until the second side is lightly charred, about 10 minutes longer.

Remove cauliflower from the oven and place it in a serving bowl. Gently toss it together with the red pepper flakes, capers and vinegar. Taste and season with any additional salt, if desired. Sprinkle chopped parsley over the cauliflower and serve immediately.

VEGGIE SIDES

SERVES
4–6

PREP TIME
10 minutes

COOK TIME
10 minutes

TOTAL TIME
20 minutes

SAUTÉED MIXED MUSHROOMS

The key to this recipe is using a large assortment of mushrooms so you get lots of different flavors and textures. Use this as an opportunity to try a variety you may have never cooked with before!

¼ cup olive oil

2 pounds assorted mushrooms, chopped or sliced into small pieces

1 teaspoon dried oregano

2 Tablespoons balsamic vinegar

1 Tablespoon soy sauce (use tamari for a gluten-free option)

Salt

Heat the oil in a large skillet over medium-high heat. Once oil is glistening, add mushrooms and cook, stirring often, for 3–4 minutes or until mushrooms begin to soften.

Sprinkle oregano over the mushrooms and add in the vinegar and soy sauce. Stir well and continue cooking another 1–2 minutes or until mushrooms are fully cooked. Taste and adjust seasonings as desired, adding more vinegar or soy sauce, or seasoning with a few pinches of salt, if desired. Serve immediately.

VEGGIE SIDES

SERVES
4

PREP TIME
5 minutes

COOK TIME
5 minutes

TOTAL TIME
10 minutes

SIMPLE GREENS

While I feel somewhat silly adding such a simple recipe to this book, I get asked all the time for this recipe when I prepare greens at retreats or for dinner guests, so it seemed essential to include it. The key to this dish is to get the oil really hot before adding greens so that they cook quickly and edges just slightly char.

1 Tablespoon coconut oil

1 bunch lacinato kale, de-ribbed and chopped into bite-sized pieces*

Salt

Heat oil in a large skillet over medium-high heat. Once oil is very hot, add the kale and a few pinches of salt and cook for 3-4 minutes or until edges are slightly charred, stirring often. Serve immediately.

This preparation works fabulously with curly kale, purple kale and collard greens as well. I don't recommend using baby kale for this recipe as it is too delicate to withstand the hot oil.

VEGGIE SIDES

MAPLE-GINGER GLAZED ACORN SQUASH

SERVES
4

PREP TIME
15 minutes

COOK TIME
1 hour

TOTAL TIME
1 hour 15 minutes

This is a staple recipe in my annual Thanksgiving cooking class. You can easily double or triple the recipe to feed a crowd.

1 large acorn squash

Olive oil

3 Tablespoons butter (use vegan butter for vegan option)

3 Tablespoons maple syrup

½-inch piece ginger, peeled and finely grated

Salt and pepper

Preheat oven to 375 degrees. Line a small baking sheet with parchment paper and lightly brush with olive oil.

Cut acorn squash into halves and use a spoon to scoop out the seeds and pulp. Once cleaned, cut each half into quarters. Place the squash cut-side up on the prepared baking sheet, and lightly season with salt and pepper.

In a small saucepan, combine butter, maple syrup and ginger. Cook over medium heat until bubbling, and then lower heat and cook about 3 minutes longer. The glaze should thicken slightly during cooking and should be a uniform color when ready.

Brush squash generously with the glaze (being sure to reserve some glaze for later) and place tray into the oven. Cook for about 1 hour total, or until squash is tender and edges are lightly browned, brushing with more glaze at the 20- and 40-minute marks. Transfer squash to a platter and serve immediately.

VEGGIE SIDES

TURMERIC SWEET POTATO HASH

SERVES
4–6

This easy hash is beautiful in color and is a great accompaniment to any meal, including savory breakfasts. Be sure to cut the sweet potatoes as uniformly as possible so they cook evenly.

PREP TIME
15 minutes

COOK TIME
30 minutes

TOTAL TIME
45 minutes

2 Tablespoons coconut oil

1 small red onion, diced

1 small red bell pepper, diced

¾ teaspoon turmeric powder

2–3 sweet potatoes (about 1½ pounds), peeled and diced into ¼-inch cubes

½ teaspoon salt

Melt coconut oil in a large skillet over medium-high heat. Add onion and pepper and cook until soft, about 5–6 minutes. Stir in turmeric and cook an additional 30 seconds; then add in sweet potatoes and mix to coat them with the sautéed onions and peppers. Cook hash for 20–25 minutes, stirring often, until sweet potatoes are tender. Stir in salt, adding more to taste if desired. Serve immediately.

VEGGIE SIDES

SERVES
4-6

MAPLE-BALSAMIC BRUSSELS SPROUTS

PREP TIME
10 minutes

COOK TIME
10 minutes

TOTAL TIME
20 minutes

I am quite lucky to be married to someone who is great in the kitchen. This is one of my husband's creations that I've incorporated into my own repertoire. I challenge anyone who thinks they don't like Brussels sprouts to try these and prepare to be delighted.

1 pound Brussels sprouts

2 Tablespoons olive oil

2 Tablespoons maple syrup

1 Tablespoon balsamic vinegar

Salt and pepper

Prepare Brussels sprouts by chopping off all the stems and then slicing each sprout in half through the stem end. If you are working with particularly large sprouts, you will want to quarter them so that they cook efficiently.

In a large skillet (with enough room for sprouts to fit in a single layer), heat olive oil over medium-high heat. Once oil is hot, add Brussels sprouts and season lightly with salt and pepper. Sauté sprouts until the outer layers are tender, stirring often to prevent burning. Reduce heat slightly if sprouts begin to get too brown on the edges.

Add in maple syrup and vinegar, and stir to coat sprouts well. Continue cooking until sprouts are fork-tender all the way through. Add more salt, maple syrup and/or vinegar to taste. Serve immediately.

HORSERADISH MASHED POTATOES

SERVES 4–6

PREP TIME 15 minutes

COOK TIME 30 minutes

TOTAL TIME 45 minutes

A cousin of broccoli and cabbage, horseradish is one of my favorite superfoods. In this recipe, it adds nutrition and other healing benefits to a dish that is generally unimpressive from a nutritional perspective as well as a delightful pungent flavor.

1 pound Russet potatoes, peeled and chopped

1 pound Yukon gold potatoes, peeled and chopped

¾ cup whole milk (use rice milk for a vegan option)

2 Tablespoons butter (use vegan butter for a vegan option)

2 tablespoons fresh horseradish root, peeled and grated

Salt

Place potatoes in a large pot and add 1 teaspoon of salt and enough cold water to cover the potatoes by about an inch. Cover pot and bring potatoes to a boil over high heat, and then reduce heat and simmer for 20–25 minutes or until potatoes are easily pierced with a fork.

While potatoes cook, place the milk, butter, horseradish and 1¼ teaspoons salt in a small saucepan over medium-low heat. Once butter is fully melted, whisk everything together well and reduced heat to the lowest setting to keep milk mixture warm until potatoes are finished cooking.

Drain potatoes when they are ready and return them to the same pot. Use a potato masher to crush all the potatoes until they are fairly crumbly. There may still be some lumps, but that is okay. Do not over mash potatoes or they will get gummy. Add in the hot milk mixture and use a wooden spoon to mix everything together gently. Taste the potatoes and add additional salt if desired. Serve immediately or keep covered until ready to serve.

VEGGIE SIDES

SERVES
4–6

PREP TIME
20 minutes

COOK TIME
15 minutes

TOTAL TIME
35 minutes

SPICED OKRA WITH PEANUTS

This is my take on bhindi masala, one of my favorite Indian dishes. Although imported okra can often be found year-round, this is really a dish to make in the summer when okra is at its peak.

1 Tablespoon ghee (use a neutral oil for a vegan option)

½ red onion, diced

1 teaspoon garam masala

¼ teaspoon amchur powder*

1 pound okra, trimmed and quartered lengthwise**

1 Tablespoon lime juice

½ teaspoon salt

2 Tablespoons chopped roasted peanuts, plus extra for garnish

Chopped cilantro (optional)

Heat ghee/oil over medium-high heat in a large skillet. When hot, add onion and cook for 3–4 minutes, or until lightly browned. Stir in garam masala and amchur and cook for an additional 30 seconds. Add in okra and sauté, stirring often, for 5–6 minutes or until tender. Stir in lime juice, salt and peanuts, and then transfer to a serving bowl. Top okra with additional chopped peanuts and cilantro (if using) and serve immediately.

*Amchur is made of powdered dried mangoes. It can be found in Indian markets or online, and adds tart flavor to anything you use it in. If it is not available, you can add additional lime juice in its place.

**To keep okra from getting sticky, be sure your knife and cutting board stay as dry as possible throughout the slicing process. Use a towel to wipe down any wet surfaces as you work.

VEGGIE SIDES

VEGGIE SIDES

SERVES
4–6

PREP TIME
5 minutes

COOK TIME
20 minutes

TOTAL TIME
25 minutes

ROASTED BROCCOLI WITH MEYER LEMON

Roasting broccoli is my favorite way to prepare it. While it's quite good on its own with just olive oil and salt, I love adding in a sliced Meyer lemon in the spring or any other time I can get my hands on one.

1½ pounds broccoli, trimmed and cut into large florets

1 Meyer lemon, very thinly sliced (use a mandoline if you have one)

2 Tablespoons olive oil

Crushed red chile flakes

Salt

Pre-heat oven to 400 degrees.

In a large bowl, stir together broccoli, lemon slices and olive oil. Lightly season with a few pinches each of chile flakes and salt. Spread the broccoli on a large rimmed baking sheet in a single layer. Roast broccoli for 15–20 minutes or until tops and edges are lightly browned, flipping once about halfway through using a spatula. Serve immediately.

STIR-FRIED SAVOY CABBAGE & SHIITAKES

SERVES
4–6

PREP TIME
10 minutes

COOK TIME
10 minutes

TOTAL TIME
20 minutes

If you have the mistaken notion that cabbage is a "boring" vegetable or believe that recipes need to have a long ingredient list to taste good, prepare to be surprised! This simple side dish is packed full of umami goodness, thanks to shiitake mushrooms. I highly recommend using savoy cabbage if you can find it, but regular green cabbage will work just fine.

- 3 Tablespoons sesame oil, divided
- 10–12 shiitake mushrooms, sliced
- 1 head savoy cabbage, cored and sliced into very thin ribbons
- 1 Tablespoon sesame seeds
- Salt

In a large skillet (or a wok), heat 2 tablespoons of oil over medium-high heat. When hot, add mushrooms and a pinch of salt. Stir-fry for about 3 minutes, or until mushrooms are dark and glistening. Add the remaining tablespoon of oil, followed by the cabbage, sesame seeds and ¼ teaspoon of salt. Stir-fry until cabbage is soft and edges are just slightly browned. Remove from heat and serve immediately.

VEGGIE SIDES

CARROT, DAIKON & HIJIKI STIR-FRY

SERVES
4–6

PREP TIME
10 minutes

COOK TIME
10 minutes

TOTAL TIME
20 minutes

This easy stir-fry is a great accompaniment to Asian-inspired meals or can be a colorful meal of its own served over rice or soba noodles.

2 Tablespoons dried hijiki seaweed

2 Tablespoons sesame oil

1 pound carrots, grated

½ pound daikon radish, grated

2 Tablespoons soy sauce (use tamari for a gluten-free option)

1 Tablespoon sesame seeds

Place hijiki in a small bowl and cover with cold water. Let it sit for 10 minutes, then drain (I recommend doing this before grating the other vegetables).

Heat oil in a large skillet, then add carrots and daikon. Cook for 2–3 minutes, stirring frequently. Add in drained hijiki, soy sauce and sesame seeds. Cook an additional 2–3 minutes, or until carrot and daikon are at desired softness. Serve immediately.

VEGGIE SIDES

SERVES
4–6

PREP TIME
20 minutes

COOK TIME
30 minutes

TOTAL TIME
50 minutes
+ resting time

ROASTED EGGPLANT WITH CILANTRO

When a client received a bunch of eggplant and cilantro in her summertime CSA box, we came up with this recipe as a way to use it all. I sometimes add cooked black lentils to this dish for a heartier, protein-rich option.

3 large eggplants, cut into 1-inch rounds

2 Tablespoons olive oil

1 small bunch cilantro, chopped (plus additional for garnish)

2 Tablespoons rice vinegar

2 Tablespoons soy sauce (use tamari for gluten-free option)

1 pinch crushed red chile flakes

Salt

Preheat oven to 400 degrees.

Rub the sides of each eggplant round lightly with salt and place in a small bowl for 10–15 minutes. Wipe any excess liquid off the eggplant and cut each slice into 1-inch cubes. Toss eggplant with olive oil and then arrange on a large baking sheet in a single layer. Roast for 15 minutes, then flip the cubes with a spatula and bake for another 15 minutes, or until eggplant is soft and slightly crispy on the edges.

Let the eggplant cool for about 10 minutes and then place it in a medium bowl. Shake together all remaining ingredients in a small jar. Pour the dressing over the eggplant and stir well. Serve at room temperature, garnished with additional cilantro.

VEGGIE SIDES

VEGGIE SIDES

SERVES
4–6

PREP TIME
15 minutes

COOK TIME
25 minutes

TOTAL TIME
40 minutes

POTATO & GREEN BEAN SUBJI

Subji is a generic term for "vegetable" in Indian cooking, and this basic preparation technique can be applied to just about any combination of vegetables you wish to use.

2 Tablespoons ghee (or coconut oil for a vegan option)

1 Tablespoon brown mustard seeds

1-inch piece of ginger, peeled and grated

1 teaspoon turmeric powder

Two-finger pinch of hing, aka asafoetida (optional)

1 pound Yukon gold potatoes, diced into ¼-inch cubes

¼ pound green beans, trimmed and chopped

Salt

In a large skillet, melt ghee/oil over a medium flame. Add mustard seeds and cook until they begin to pop. Stir in ginger, turmeric and hing and cook for 1 minute. Add potatoes and green beans and stir well to combine. Add 1–2 tablespoons of water and then cover and cook 15–20 minutes, stirring often and adding additional water (1 tablespoon at a time) if vegetables begin to stick. Once potatoes are soft, add a few pinches of salt to taste. Serve immediately.

VEGGIE SIDES

MOROCCAN CAULIFLOWER

SERVES
6–8

I learned to make this dish from Chef Souad at Café Clock in Fes, Morocco. When we made it, everything was eyeballed and done intuitively, so feel free to taste and adjust the spices to your own liking.

PREP TIME
10 minutes

COOK TIME
50 minutes

TOTAL TIME
1 hour
+ resting time

1 large head cauliflower, chopped into large florets (~6 cups)

1 lemon, quartered

2 cloves garlic, pressed

½ cup chopped cilantro

2 teaspoons ground cumin

2 teaspoons paprika

1 teaspoon chile powder

2 Tablespoons lemon juice

⅓ cup good quality olive oil

1 teaspoon salt

Place cauliflower and the quartered lemon in a large pot and add enough water to cover everything. Bring to a boil, cover, and cook over a low flame for about 35–40 minutes or until the cauliflower is very soft. Remove lemon sections and drain cauliflower in a colander. Rinse with cold water and let it cool to room temperature.

Once cool, add all the remaining ingredients to a large bowl. Use your hands (or a spoon) to mix well; then add cauliflower and use your hands to break up the florets as you toss them with the dressing. Keep going until the cauliflower is uniformly mashed and then let it sit at least 30 minutes to allow flavors to meld before serving.

This dish can be made in advance and refrigerated (be sure to take it out at least an hour before serving and bring to room temperature).

VEGGIE SIDES

SERVES
4–6

PREP TIME
10 minutes

COOK TIME
15 minutes

TOTAL TIME
25 minutes

DIJON DILL POTATOES

These warm potatoes are tossed in a sweet and pungent dressing that both adults and kids love. This dish can also be made ahead of time as a more elegant alternative to a mayo-based potato salad.

1½ pounds Peewee potatoes

2 Tablespoons apple cider vinegar

1 Tablespoon + 1 teaspoon Dijon mustard

2½ teaspoons honey (use maple syrup for a vegan option)

¼ cup olive oil

2 Tablespoons chopped dill, plus additional for garnish

¼ teaspoon salt

Place potatoes in a medium pot and cover with water by about an inch. Add a few pinches of salt. Bring to a boil over high heat, and then cover the pot and reduce heat to low. Cook potatoes 8–10 minutes, or until fork-tender but not mushy (i.e., skins should still be intact). Drain well in a colander and let potatoes cool just slightly.

Place all remaining ingredients in a jar and shake vigorously until dressing is well emulsified. Taste and adjust flavors as desired. Pour dressing over cooled potatoes in a large bowl and stir well to coat. Top with extra dill and serve immediately or chill and serve as a potato salad.

VEGGIE SIDES

GETTING THE MOST LIFE OUT OF FRESH HERBS

In the cooking classes I offer, people often bemoan how quickly their fresh herbs will turn brown and go bad. This challenge is common because herbs are usually sold in fairly sizeable bundles, and recipes will often call for only a very small amount. Many people just store the herbs in a plastic produce bag or in whatever packaging they came in, and that is often part of the problem. Here are a few tips to help you get the most life out of your herbs:

· · · Hardier herbs (i.e., anything with a bit of a woodier stem; think rosemary, thyme, sage, and oregano) will do best wrapped in a thin kitchen towel or paper towel and stored in a bag or other sealed container in the refrigerator. The towel will wick away any excess moisture that accumulates.

· · · More delicate herbs, such as mint, parsley, and cilantro, will enjoy the longest life when stored in water. Fill a small glass or mason jar with a couple inches of water, and then place the herbs inside. Cover the jar top-down with a plastic bag, carefully gather the bag opening under the bottom of the jar to keep air out (or use a rubber band around the neck of the jar), and then refrigerate. Replace the water every 2-3 days, and be very careful not to knock over the jar when grabbing other items from the fridge.

· · · For basil, use a similar method to that for delicate herbs, but cover the jar loosely with a bag and leave it on the countertop in a cool place that is out of direct sunlight.

· · · Wash only what you need, when you need it. I often see people wash a whole bunch of herbs, pick off what they need, and then try to store the rest. The excess water makes the herbs' survival extremely difficult, so avoid doing this.

MOROCCAN DATE CAKE

CHOCOLATE AVOCADO PUDDING

THE PERFECT DATE

THE MOST PERFECT DATE

ORANGE POPPY SEED PUDDING

EASY PEACH COBBLER

RAW PIÑA COLADA "CHEESE" CAKE

BLOOD ORANGE & THYME SORBET

CASHEW CRÈME

DESSERT

SERVES
6

PREP TIME
20 minutes

COOK TIME
45 minutes

TOTAL TIME
1 hour
5 minutes

MOROCCAN DATE CAKE

This elegant cake features one of my favorite flavor combinations: orange and clove. It is super moist and works well with one-to-one gluten-free flour mixes.

½ pound Medjool dates, pitted and roughly chopped

1 cup water

1 teaspoon baking soda

¾ cup coconut sugar

1 stick (¼ pound) butter (or vegan butter), softened

2 eggs or 2 prepared flax eggs (see p. 208)

Zest of 1 orange

1¼ cups unbleached all-purpose flour (or gluten-free flour mix)

½ teaspoon ground clove

2 teaspoons baking powder

¾ cup chopped walnuts (optional)

Orange slices or segments (for garnish/serving)

In a small saucepan, bring dates and water to a boil over high heat. Once boiling, add baking soda (mixture will foam) and reduce heat to low. Gently simmer for 1 minute, then remove date mixture from heat and set aside to let it cool slightly.

Pre-heat oven to 350 degrees. Line the bottom of a 9-inch springform pan with parchment and lightly oil the walls of the pan.

DESSERT

In a large mixing bowl, beat together coconut sugar and butter using a hand mixer; then, beat in eggs and orange zest. Add dates and cooking liquid to the bowl, and mix well. In a small bowl, whisk together flour, clove and baking powder, then add to the wet mixture and mix until just combined. Fold in nuts, if using.

Place batter in the prepared pan. Bake for 35-45 minutes, or until an inserted toothpick comes out clean. Let cake cool at least 20 minutes before releasing the springform ring. Serve cake with optional citrus garnish.

DESSERT

SERVES
2–4

PREP TIME
5 minutes

TOTAL TIME
5 minutes
+ chill time

CHOCOLATE AVOCADO PUDDING

This easy, no-cook pudding also makes a great cake frosting or fruit dip. Truth be told, it's good on just about anything sweet!

2 ripe avocados

3 dates, pitted, soaked at least 15 minutes and drained (reserve liquid)

2 Tablespoons date soaking water (plus more if needed)

¼ cup maple syrup

¼ teaspoon vanilla extract

1/3 cup raw cacao powder

Cacao nibs for garnish (optional)

Combine all ingredients in a high-powered blender. Use a tamper to aid processing if you have one, or else scrape down the sides often until pudding is smooth and creamy. (Add a small amount of additional date soaking water if needed to assist processing.)

Taste, and if you'd like a sweeter pudding, you can add a bit more maple syrup. Transfer to 2 or more dessert dishes and chill until ready to serve (I recommend chilling at least 2–3 hours because the pudding is generally a bit warm after being blended). Garnish individual portions with a sprinkle of cacao nibs if you wish.

DESSERT

THE PERFECT DATE

SERVES
6

PREP TIME
15 minutes

TOTAL TIME
15 minutes

These sweet nibbles were inspired by my friend Jill, who used to prepare something very similar on retreats we worked at together. I love serving these on a platter sprinkled with rose petals for a beautiful presentation. (P.S. Dates do get more perfect—see the next page!)

12 dates (any variety), cut in half and pitted

¼ cup cashew butter or tahini

1 teaspoon ground cardamom

1 teaspoon honey (or maple syrup for a vegan option)

A couple drops of rosewater

24 raw cacao nibs (optional)

In a small bowl, mix cashew butter (or tahini), cardamom, honey (or maple syrup) and rosewater together well. Give it a taste and feel free to add more of any of the ingredients to suit your taste.

Use your fingers or a small spoon to stuff filling into each date half and smooth the surface. Lightly press a cacao nib on the top of each stuffed date, if using. Serve immediately or refrigerate prior to serving. Dates can be made a day or two prior to serving.

DESSERT

THE MOST PERFECT DATE

SERVES
10

PREP TIME
25 minutes

TOTAL TIME
25 minutes
+ freezing

I learned to make these in a rooftop cooking class in Morocco, using exquisitely fresh dates that had just been procured in the market below us. They have quickly become a hit with my clients, some of whom order batches of them at a time—so much so that I had to come up with a superlative title for them since I thought I had already found a perfect date (see the previous recipe)! If you are familiar with tempering chocolate (or want to Google it and learn), feel free to use that procedure to create a harder shell that melts less easily. I've included the directions I learned in Morocco for a quicker preparation.

20 Medjool dates

10 whole walnuts, broken into halves

2 Tablespoons orange blossom water*

1/2 pound good-quality dark chocolate

¼ cup unsalted pistachios or roasted almonds

¼ teaspoon dried rose petals (optional)

ORANGE BLOSSOM WATER can be found at Middle Eastern markets or ordered online.

Use a knife to make a slit lengthwise along each date. Unfold the date slightly to remove the pit, then insert half of a walnut and press the date back together to assume its original shape. Once all dates have been pitted and stuffed, place them in a small bowl with the orange blossom water. Let dates sit for 10–15 minutes.

While the dates soak, prepare the chocolate in a double boiler (or by setting a smaller pan above a larger pan of boiling water). Stir chocolate until it melts and is smooth. You may add up to a tablespoon of hot water to help thin the chocolate. Turn off heat and let chocolate sit above the hot water until you're ready to assemble your dates.

Prepare topping by whizzing together pistachios (or almonds) and rose petals (if using) in a mini food processor or blender until fairly finely chopped. Transfer topping to a small bowl. Once the dates are done soaking, drain them well. Line a small cookie sheet or baking dish with parchment or waxed paper. To cover dates in chocolate, dip a spoon into the chocolate and then place a date on the spoon. Use a fork to rotate the date around until it is fully covered in chocolate and gently place it on the lined tray/dish. Sprinkle with topping. Repeat the process for each remaining date.

Once all dates have been prepared, place the tray/dish in the freezer for at least 2 hours. Dates are best kept frozen until you're ready to serve them and can be made a day or two in advance and stored in a sealed container in the freezer.

DESSERT

SERVES
4

PREP TIME
5 minutes

COOK TIME
15 minutes

TOTAL TIME
20 minutes
+ soak time

ORANGE POPPY SEED PUDDING

Puddings are often prepared in Ayurvedic cooking because they are generally easy to digest. With chewy tapioca and crunchy poppy seeds, this pudding's texture is as delightful as its flavor.

½ cup tapioca pearls (not quick-cooking variety)

3½ cups almond milk, divided

½ cup maple syrup

Zest of 2 oranges (~2 teaspoons)

1½ teaspoons poppy seeds

½ teaspoon almond extract

¼ teaspoon salt

Quartered orange slice for garnish

Place tapioca pearls in a small bowl with 1½ cups almond milk and let them soak for 3-4 hours minimum (or overnight).

Place soaked tapioca pearls and any excess soaking liquid in a medium saucepan, along with the remaining 2 cups of almond milk. Bring the mixture to a boil over medium heat and then stir in the maple syrup. Wait for the mixture to return to a boil. Turn heat to low and stir continuously for 8 minutes. Stir in orange zest, poppy seeds, almond extract, and salt and cook for another 3 minutes while stirring.

Divide warm pudding between four ramekins or small bowls and refrigerate at least 2 hours before serving. Garnish with quartered orange slices when serving.

DESSERT

EASY PEACH COBBLER

SERVES
8–10

PREP TIME
20 minutes

COOK TIME
40 minutes

TOTAL TIME
1 hour

This cobbler is a part of just about every summer retreat menu I prepare. In the fall, I often replace the peaches with chopped apples and a handful of cranberries for an autumnal variation. The pecans can be omitted from the topping if you are cooking for anyone with a nut allergy.

3½ pounds ripe peaches, washed, halved and sliced

½ pound pitted dates

2 cups quick oats (certified gluten-free if necessary)

½ cup quinoa flakes (or use an additional ½ cup of oats)

½ cup chopped pecans

¼ cup coconut oil, melted

Pinch of salt

Cashew crème for serving – see p. 174

Preheat oven to 375 degrees. Lightly oil a 9x13" baking dish. Arrange peach slices in even layers in pan.

Add dates to a food processor and pulse a few times to begin to break up dates. Add oats and quinoa flakes and continuing pulsing until dates are uniformly crumbly and incorporated. Transfer date mixture to a medium-sized mixing bowl, and add pecans, oil and salt. Stir well. Then place date-oat mixture on top of the peaches, using a rubber spatula to smooth the topping evenly.

Bake cobbler 30–40 minutes until topping is golden brown. Let cobbler cool at least 15 minutes before serving. Serve individual portions of cobbler with a dollop of cashew crème.

DESSERT

SERVES
8

PREP TIME
20 minutes

TOTAL TIME
20 minutes
+ soaking & freezing

RAW PIÑA COLADA "CHEESE" CAKE

I love making raw desserts, especially on hot summer days when I can't bear the thought of turning on my oven. I've had success substituting strawberries or blueberries in place of the pineapple, so feel free to be adventurous with the fruit that you use.

Crust Ingredients:

⅔ cup nuts, soaked 3–4 hours and drained*

1½ cups Medjool dates, pitted

Filling Ingredients:

1½ cups raw cashews, soaked 3–4 hours and drained

1½ cups pineapple, cut into 1-inch cubes

½ cup lemon juice

½ cup coconut water

¼ cup coconut butter

¼ cup coconut oil

1 teaspoon vanilla extract

2 Tablespoons raw honey (or maple syrup for a vegan option)

⅛ teaspoon turmeric powder (optional, for color)

Pineapple slices for garnish

DESSERT

Crust Preparation:
Process the nuts in a food processor until crumbly. Add the dates (the food processor may "jump" a bit when you add the dates, so be prepared to hold the base down) and continue to process until a crumbly yet generally even texture is achieved. Press this mixture into the pie pan, using your fingers to mold it into the shape of the pan. (If you are using a shallower pie pan and have leftover crust mixture, you can form it into balls and refrigerate for a sweet snack.)

Filling Preparation:
Process all filling ingredients in a blender until very smooth. Place filling in the crust and chill in the freezer at least 2-3 hours before serving. Allow about 20 minutes to thaw slightly before serving. Garnish with thinly sliced pineapple.

*I like to use Brazil nuts and almonds; cashews, pecans and walnuts are great too

DESSERT

SERVES
6–8

PREP TIME
20 minutes

PROCESSING TIME
1 hour

TOTAL TIME
1 hour
20 minutes
+ chilling time

BLOOD ORANGE & THYME SORBET

The dark ruby color of blood orange juice makes for a visually striking sorbet with an herbal kick. If you don't have an ice cream maker, you can easily make more of a granita-style dessert by freezing the mix in a large baking dish and running a fork across it every hour for about six hours.

4 cups fresh-squeezed blood orange juice

1 cup maple syrup

½ cup prosecco

2 Tablespoons fresh thyme leaves

Blood orange slices and/or thyme sprigs for serving

Mix all ingredients together well in a blender (or place in a large bowl and use an immersion blender). Transfer mix to a large jar or container and chill in the refrigerator for at least an hour. Then pour mix into an ice cream maker and run machine according to manufacturer's instructions.

Place finished sorbet in a sealed freezer-safe container until ready to serve. Garnish as desired with sliced blood orange and/or thyme sprigs.

DESSERT

SERVES
4–6

PREP TIME
5 minutes

TOTAL TIME
5 minutes
+ soaking

CASHEW CRÈME

This versatile dessert can be used as a dip for fresh fruit or as a substitute for traditional whipped cream. It is a favorite on retreats, and it's not uncommon for someone to grab a rubber spatula and scrape every last drop out of the bowl. It's also a particular hit with kids.

2 cups raw cashews, soaked min. 2 hours and drained

¼ cup maple syrup

½ teaspoon vanilla bean powder (or 1 teaspoon vanilla extract)

½ cup coconut water

Blend everything together in a high-speed blender until a smooth, creamy consistency is achieved. Add a bit more coconut water as needed while blending to aid processing or for a thinner consistency.

DESSERT

· · VARIATIONS · ·

Add a couple pinches of ground cardamom and/or a drop or two of rosewater

. . . .

Add ~2 teaspoons raw cacao powder, along with 1 additional teaspoon of maple syrup

. . . .

Add a pinch or two of cinnamon

. . . .

TEAS & SMOOTHIES

PRANAFUL CHAI

MOROCCAN MINT TEA

CORIANDER, FENNEL & CUMIN TEA

HEARTWARMER TEA

GOLDEN ROSE MILK

LEMON VERBENA & MINT TEA

MATCHA LATTE

TROPICAL GREEN SMOOTHIE

HEMP PROTEIN SMOOTHIE

DATE SHAKE

TEAS & SMOOTHIES

PRANAFUL CHAI

SERVES 6

PREP TIME 5 minutes

COOK TIME 50 minutes

TOTAL TIME 55 minutes + overnight

On my first trip to India, I was terribly disappointed to learn that most people there make chai using stale powdered spices and tons of sugar. I've since stuck to making chai my way, using whole spices including licorice root, which gives the tea a sweet flavor without added sugar.

2 Tablespoons green cardamom pods

2 Tablespoons fennel seeds

1 Tablespoon chopped dried licorice root

1 teaspoon whole cloves

1 teaspoon black peppercorns

2 cinnamon sticks

8 pieces star anise

2-inch piece of fresh ginger, peeled and chopped into thin rounds

3 cups water

3 Tablespoons black tea in a large tea ball or 3 black tea bags

3 cups coconut milk (or other milk of your choice)

Honey or other sweetener of your choice (optional)

Add all dry spices to a medium pot and toast them over a medium flame, stirring often to avoid burning. When spices become aromatic, add ginger and water, and then turn heat to high and bring to a boil. Reduce heat to low and simmer for 20–30 minutes, covered. Turn off heat, and leave spices to steep overnight in the covered pot.

The next morning, bring the spice decoction to a boil over a high flame. Remove from heat, and add tea ball/bags. Let tea steep for 5 minutes, and then remove tea ball/bags and strain the tea. Return chai to the stove over a low flame, and stir in milk. After about 5 minutes, the chai will be ready to serve.

If you wish, sweeten individual servings with honey or a sweetener of your choice.

TEAS & SMOOTHIES

SERVES
4

PREP TIME
10 minutes

TOTAL TIME
10 minutes

MOROCCAN MINT TEA

My favorite pastime in Morocco is sitting in sidewalk cafes, sipping on mint tea while I watch people and traffic stream by. Moroccans drink their tea in small decorated heatproof glasses, which you can easily find online if you want to serve the tea in a traditional style. It is typical for Moroccan tea to be extremely sweet, but I generally enjoy it unsweetened or with just a touch of honey.

4 cups water

1 teaspoon gunpowder green tea

1 large handful fresh mint (leaves and stems)

Honey or other sweetener of your choice (optional)

Heat water to around 180 degrees (do not fully boil).

Place the tea in a teapot roughly 1-quart in size. Pour about half a cup of water into the pot and gently swirl to rinse and wake up the tea leaves. Discard the rinsing water, and then add the remaining water to the pot along with the mint.

Let the tea steep for 2–3 minutes, then serve immediately or strain. Do not oversteep the tea, or it will become bitter. Serve tea with honey or another sweetener if you wish. You can make up to 3-4 additional pots by adding more water and steeping.

CORIANDER, FENNEL & CUMIN TEA

SERVES
4

PREP TIME
5 minutes

COOK TIME
35 minutes

TOTAL TIME
40 minutes

This tea is a traditional Ayurvedic brew that is used to boost digestion and curb cravings for snacks between meals.

1 Tablespoon coriander seeds

1 Tablespoon fennel seeds

1 teaspoon cumin seeds

4 cups water

Add all ingredients to a medium pot. Bring to a boil over high heat, then simmer for 20–30 minutes. Strain tea and discard seeds. Serve immediately, or enjoy individual servings throughout the day.

HEARTWARMER TEA

SERVES
4

PREP TIME
5 minutes

COOK TIME
15 minutes

TOTAL TIME
20 minutes

This warming tea has a beautiful ruby color, thanks to blood orange.

2 cinnamon sticks

½ nutmeg seed

3 Tablespoons pau d'arco*

3 slices dried blood orange**

4 cups water

Add all ingredients to a medium pot. Bring to a boil over high heat, and then simmer for about 10 minutes at lower heat. Strain tea before serving.

*Pau d'arco is an herb taken from the inner bark of a tree found in Latin America. Among its many benefits, it has been found to boost immune response. It can be found online if your local health food store or herb shop does not carry it.

**I recommend buying extra blood oranges in the winter when they are readily available and dehydrating a stash for use year-round. If you miss the window of availability or can't find them in your area, they can be ordered online.

TEAS & SMOOTHIES

SERVES
4–6

PREP TIME
5 minutes

COOK TIME
15 minutes

TOTAL TIME
20 minutes

GOLDEN ROSE MILK

Warm turmeric milk has been used in Ayurveda for centuries to treat a host of common health issues. This blend is specially formulated to promote relaxation and good sleep. I recommend drinking a small cup as a bedtime elixir.

- 2 cups almond or hazelnut milk (or milk of your choice)
- 2 dates, pitted
- ¼ teaspoon turmeric powder
- 1/8 teaspoon ashwagandha powder* (optional)
- 4–5 drops rosewater

Place milk, dates, turmeric and ashwagandha (if using) in a small pot and bring to a gentle simmer. Cook for 10 minutes. Place spiced milk and rosewater in a blender. Vent the blender lid slightly to release steam and carefully blend at high speed until dates are fully incorporated. Serve immediately or refrigerate and reheat individual servings.

Ashwagandha is a powdered root that is heavily used in Ayurvedic medicine. It promotes sleep and revitalizes the body. It can now be commonly found at health food stores or ordered online.

TEAS & SMOOTHIES

LEMON VERBENA & MINT TEA

SERVES
4

PREP TIME
15 minutes

TOTAL TIME
15 minutes

This simple tea combines two of my favorite herbs to create a delicious brew that is cooling and especially good for the summertime. Lemon verbena is incredibly hearty and easy to grow, so if you garden, I suggest cultivating your own.

4 cups water

1 large handful fresh mint (leaves and stems)

1 handful fresh lemon verbena (or 1 Tablespoon dried)

Honey or other sweetener of your choice (optional)

Bring water to a boil.

Place mint and lemon verbena in a teapot roughly 1-quart in size. Pour water over the herbs and let the tea steep for 10 minutes. Serve immediately or strain. Serve tea with honey or another sweetener if you wish. You can make 1–2 additional pots by adding more water and steeping.

TEAS & SMOOTHIES

MATCHA LATTE

The key to a good homemade matcha latte is the equipment. If you enjoy making these, it is worth investing in a small bamboo matcha whisk (known as a *chasen*) as well as a handheld milk frother (like the Aerolatte).

1 cup water

¾ cup almond milk (or milk of your choice)

½ teaspoon matcha powder

½ teaspoon maple syrup

Heat water to around 180 degrees (do not fully boil).

Place the milk in a small saucepan and warm it gently over low heat.

Place matcha powder in a small bowl (if it is clumpy, sift it gently through a small fine-mesh strainer). Pour water over the matcha and use a matcha whisk (or a small regular whisk) in a back-and-forth pattern to mix the two together (do not make circles). Continue whisking for about 30 seconds or until the surface of the matcha is slightly frothy.

Transfer the matcha to a large mug and stir in the maple syrup. Use a handheld frother or a whisk to gently froth the milk, and then add it gently to the matcha. Serve immediately.

G **V**

SERVES
1

PREP TIME
10 minutes

TOTAL TIME
10 minutes

TEAS & SMOOTHIES

SERVES
2

PREP TIME
5 minutes

TOTAL TIME
5 minutes

TROPICAL GREEN SMOOTHIE

I've made countless varieties of green smoothies, but this one is the most inviting for people who prefer their smoothies not to taste too green. For a thinner smoothie, let the frozen fruit defrost slightly or use fresh fruit in its place.

1½ cups coconut water

½ cup almond or coconut milk

1 large handful frozen mango

1 large handful frozen pineapple

1 banana, broken into chunks

1 kiwi, peeled and chopped

2 handfuls baby spinach

1 handful kale

Place all ingredients in a blender in the order listed. Process until very smooth. Serve immediately.

TEAS & SMOOTHIES

HEMP PROTEIN SMOOTHIE

SERVES
2

PREP TIME
5 minutes

TOTAL TIME
5 minutes

This smoothie is loaded with protein and is great for people who don't like very sweet smoothies. I love this one after a morning workout or yoga session. For a thicker smoothie, freeze the banana chunks in advance.

- 2 cups almond milk
- 2 bananas, broken into chunks
- 2 Tablespoons (heaping) almond butter
- 1 Tablespoon hempseed powder
- 1 Tablespoon chia seeds
- 2 handfuls kale

Place all ingredients in a blender in the order listed. Process until very smooth. Serve immediately.

DATE SHAKE

SERVES
1

PREP TIME
5 minutes

TOTAL TIME
5 minutes

This recipe is inspired by the roadside cafés that serve up cool treats to thirsty travelers passing through the Palm Desert in California.

- 4 Medjool dates, pitted and soaked at least 30 minutes in ¼ cup warm water
- 1 cup almond milk (or milk of your choice)
- ¼ cup coconut water
- ¼ teaspoon vanilla bean powder (or substitute 1/2 teaspoon vanilla extract)
- 1 small ripe banana

Place all ingredients in a blender (including date soaking water) and process until dates are broken up and a creamy consistency is achieved.

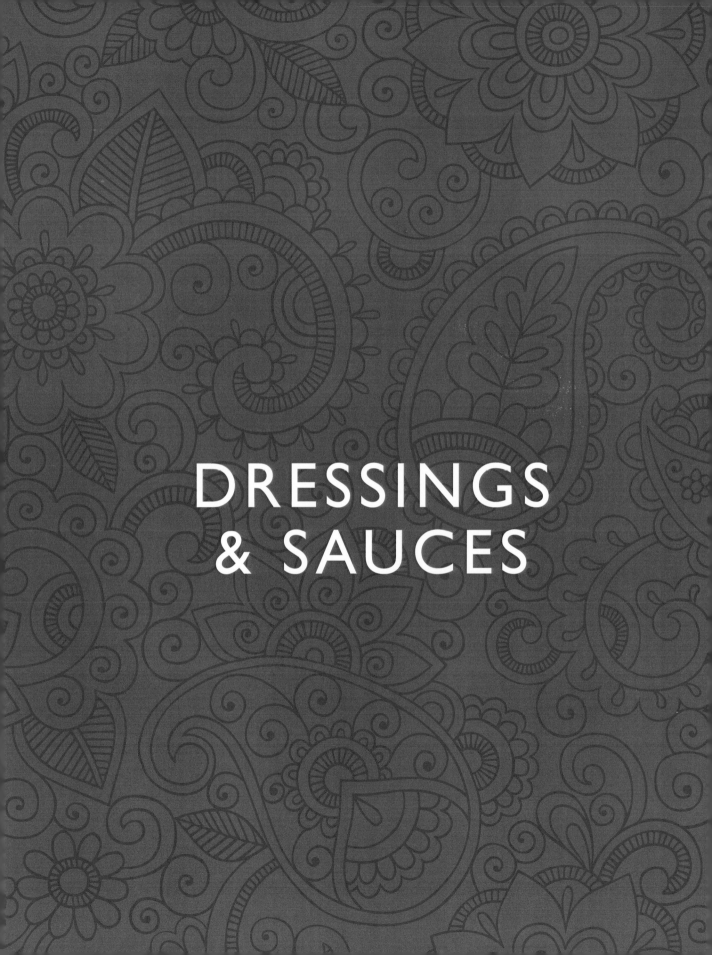

DRESSINGS & SAUCES

- TOMATILLO CHIPOTLE SALSA
- BASIL DANDELION PESTO
- ROMESCO SAUCE
- CHIMICHURRI
- GREMOLATA
- CHARMOULA
- HARISSA
- TAHINI GARLIC DRESSING
- CHIPOTLE CASHEW CREAM
- MANGO GINGER CHUTNEY
- CILANTRO COCONUT CHUTNEY
- PRESERVED LEMON DRESSING
- PERSIMMON VINAIGRETTE
- ORANGE CILANTRO DRESSING
- PARSLEY PECAN DRESSING

DRESSINGS & SAUCES

TOMATILLO CHIPOTLE SALSA

YIELD
about 1 pint

PREP TIME
10 minutes

COOK TIME
15 minutes

TOTAL TIME
25 minutes
+ resting time

This salsa comes via my dear sister, Elaine. She's made it for as long as I can remember and I've co-opted it as my own go-to salsa.

1 pound tomatillos, husked and quartered

4 cloves garlic, peeled and halved

1–2 chipotle chiles in adobo sauce

2 Tablespoons water

Salt

Heat a large skillet (cast iron is best if you have one) over a high flame. Add tomatillos, cut-side down, along with garlic. When tomatillos are lightly blackened, flip to place the opposite cut side down, and turn garlic cloves. After the second side is sufficiently blackened, place them peel side down and cook another 2–3 minutes, or until peels begin to shrivel slightly.

Place tomatillos and garlic in food processor bowl and let them cool slightly. Add chipotle and water. Process until a uniformly smooth salsa is achieved, adding more water as you go if you prefer a thinner consistency. Taste and add additional chipotles or a spoonful of adobo sauce if you want more heat. After desired heat is achieved, add in a few pinches of salt to taste and pulse a few times.

Transfer salsa to a jar or other sealed container and let it rest at least one hour before serving. Salsa will keep up to 1 week in the refrigerator.

DRESSINGS & SAUCES

YIELD
about 1¼ cup

PREP TIME
10 minutes

TOTAL TIME
10 minutes

BASIL DANDELION PESTO

Raw vegan pestos such as this one have myriad uses, from being a pasta accompaniment to a dip at a party. You can easily substitute other herbs or greens and use various nuts or seeds in place of the ones I use here. All measurements are approximate, so feel free to improvise a bit and make this recipe all your own.

¾ cup walnuts or pumpkin seeds (or a mix of both)

1 clove garlic

Juice of 1 large lemon

About 3 cups packed basil leaves

About 2 cups packed dandelion greens

¼ cup good quality olive oil

¼ cup nutritional yeast

½ teaspoon salt

Place nuts/seeds and garlic in food processor bowl and process until crumbly. Add lemon juice and pulse a few times to combine. Add greens, and process slowly while drizzling in olive oil. The oil should help the greens integrate. Stop the machine occasionally and scrape down the sides, adding a bit more olive oil as needed to help greens process.

Once desired texture is achieved, add nutritional yeast and salt and process for a few seconds, until well combined. Use pesto immediately or refrigerate until ready to serve to maintain its color.

DRESSINGS & SAUCES

ROMESCO SAUCE

YIELD
about 1½ cups

PREP TIME
10 minutes

COOK TIME
15 minutes

TOTAL TIME
25 minutes
+ cooling time

This Spanish nut and pepper sauce is one of the biggest hits from a sauce class that I offer. It perks up any vegetable with flavor and color.

¼ cup raw hazelnuts

¼ cup raw almonds

2–3 roasted red bell peppers, peeled and seeded

½ cup diced fire-roasted tomatoes

2 Tablespoons sherry vinegar*

1 Tablespoon smoked paprika

1 teaspoon chile powder

1–2 cloves garlic

¾ cup good quality olive oil

Salt & pepper

Preheat oven or toaster oven to 350 degrees.

Place hazelnuts on a rimmed baking sheet in a single layer and toast for 8–10 minutes, or until fragrant and noticeably darker. Transfer hazelnuts to the center of a clean dishtowel. Place almonds on the same tray and toast them for 4–5 minutes, or until fragrant. Wrap the towel around the hazelnuts and use your hands to slough the skins off the nuts (it's okay if some skin remains).

Once nuts are all slightly cooled, process all ingredients except olive oil in a food processor until well-pureed. Slowly drizzle in olive oil; add salt and pepper to taste. Use immediately or refrigerate in a tightly sealed jar or container.

Romesco sauce will keep for up to 10 days in the refrigerator.

Red wine vinegar can be used, but I prefer this sauce with sherry vinegar.

DRESSINGS & SAUCES

YIELD
about 1½ cups

PREP TIME
10 minutes

TOTAL TIME
10 minutes
+ resting time

CHIMICHURRI

This is my take on the Argentinian classic. Although typically served with meat, I find chimichurri is delightful on just about any roasted vegetable.

1 cup packed Italian parsley leaves

½ cup packed cilantro leaves and stems

2 Tablespoons fresh oregano leaves

⅓ cup olive oil

¼ cup sherry vinegar

1 teaspoon ground cumin

¾ teaspoon crushed red chile flakes

½ teaspoon salt

Wash and finely chop all herbs. Place in a bowl or jar and add all remaining ingredients. Stir well or shake. Let chimichurri sit a minimum of 2 hours prior to serving.

Chimichurri can be made up to 1 day in advance and refrigerated.

DRESSINGS & SAUCES

GREMOLATA

It always amazes me how simple ingredients can come together to create truly amazing flavors. This classic Italian condiment is a perfect example. I love tossing it with sautéed or stewed greens.

½ cup parsley leaves, finely chopped

2 Tablespoons olive oil

Juice and zest of one large lemon

1 clove garlic, finely minced

Pinch of crushed red chile flakes (optional)

2 large pinches salt

Whisk together all ingredients in a small bowl. Adjust salt to taste. Use gremolata immediately or within 2-3 hours of preparation.

YIELD
about ⅔ cup

PREP TIME
10 minutes

TOTAL TIME
10 minutes

CHARMOULA

This pungent Moroccan herb sauce is great on carrots or any other hearty vegetable.

1 small bunch cilantro leaves and stems, chopped

1 large handful Italian parsley leaves, chopped

1 clove garlic, grated on a Microplane

½ preserved lemon (rind only), finely chopped

1 teaspoon smoked paprika

½ teaspoon ground cumin

¼ teaspoon salt

2 Tablespoons lemon juice

2 Tablespoons olive oil

Mix all ingredients together in a medium bowl. Adjust seasonings as desired. Use charmoula immediately or refrigerate and use within 24 hours.

YIELD
about ½ cup

PREP TIME
10 minutes

TOTAL TIME
10 minutes

HARISSA

YIELD
about 1 cup

PREP TIME
15 minutes

COOK TIME
5 minutes

TOTAL TIME
20 minutes
+ resting time

Harissa is a condiment used widely in North African cuisine. It livens up any meal in addition to making an excellent sandwich spread.

2 large dried ancho chiles

6 sun-dried tomatoes (dry-packed, not in oil)

2 teaspoons coriander seeds

1 teaspoon caraway seeds

¾ teaspoon cumin seeds

1 small roasted red bell pepper, skin and seeds removed

½ teaspoon paprika

1–2 cloves garlic, roughly chopped

Zest of one small lemon

1 Tablespoon olive oil, plus additional for storage

1 teaspoon tomato paste

¼ teaspoon salt

Place ancho chiles and sun-dried tomatoes in a small bowl and cover with boiling water. Set aside for at least 15 minutes to soak.

Heat a small skillet over medium flame. Once hot, gently toast coriander, caraway and cumin seeds. Remove from heat and, once cool, use a spice grinder or mortar and pestle to create a spice powder.

Drain the chiles and sun-dried tomatoes, reserving the soaking liquid. In a small food processor or blender, puree the chiles, sun-dried tomatoes, roasted red bell pepper and 1 tablespoon of soaking liquid until smooth. Add the ground spices along with all other ingredients and pulse a few times to mix well. Adjust salt or other spices as you wish, and then use immediately or transfer to a small jar for storage. Top the harissa with a thin layer of olive oil to prevent mold from growing. Harissa will last 1–2 months in the refrigerator.

DRESSINGS & SAUCES

TAHINI GARLIC DRESSING

YIELD
about 1¼ cups

PREP TIME
10 minutes

TOTAL TIME
10 minutes

You'll never want to eat a bottled dressing again after tasting this oil-free dressing. I get more requests for this recipe than just about anything else I make.

¼ cup tahini

1 cup water

¼ cup nutritional yeast

1 Tablespoon smooth Dijon mustard

1 clove garlic, grated on a Microplane

¼ teaspoon salt

Whisk together all ingredients in a small bowl. Add 1–2 additional tablespoons of water as needed to thin the dressing as desired. Taste and adjust salt or other ingredients as desired before serving. The longer you let this dressing sit, the thicker it becomes, so you may need to add additional water just before serving or when using leftover portions. This dressing will keep for up to 10–12 days in the refrigerator.

CHIPOTLE CASHEW CREAM

YIELD
about 1½ cups

PREP TIME
10 minutes

TOTAL TIME
10 minutes

This sauce is great on tacos or drizzled over roasted potatoes. Use it in place of sour cream in any Mexican-themed dishes.

1 cup raw cashews, soaked 4–6 hours and drained

¼ cup lemon juice

1 chipotle pepper in adobo sauce

½ cup water

¼ teaspoon salt

Combine all ingredients in blender until smooth. Add additional water 1 tablespoon at a time (if needed) to achieve a creamy consistency. Serve immediately or refrigerate in a tightly-sealed jar or container until ready to serve. Cashew cream will keep for 5–7 days in the refrigerator.

DRESSINGS & SAUCES

MANGO GINGER CHUTNEY

G V

While technically a condiment, this chutney is so delicious you may find yourself reaching for a spoon and eating it as a snack.

- 2 large ripe mangoes, chopped
- 1-inch piece of ginger, grated or chopped finely
- ¼ cup apple cider vinegar
- ¼ cup maple syrup

Bring all ingredients to a boil in a small saucepan, then simmer for 20 minutes over low heat, stirring occasionally. Let chutney cool completely, then transfer to a jar or container. Serve chutney once it is cooled or cover and refrigerate for later use.

This chutney will keep for up to 2 weeks in the refrigerator.

YIELD
about 1 pint

PREP TIME
10 minutes

COOK TIME
20 minutes

TOTAL TIME
30 minutes

CILANTRO COCONUT CHUTNEY

G V

This chutney is a staple in the seasonal cleanses I lead each year and often is participants' favorite dish. You can substitute a mix of mint and parsley in place of cilantro if you are averse to it.

- 1 bunch of cilantro (leaves and upper stems), chopped
- ¼ cup lime juice
- ½ cup dried coconut flakes (unsweetened)
- 1 Tablespoon honey (use maple syrup for a vegan option)
- ½ teaspoon salt

Blend all ingredients in a blender or food processor until everything is well integrated (add a few tablespoons of water if things are not processing well). You will likely need to stop the machine and scrape down the sides to achieve a good consistency. Use immediately or refrigerate in a tightly sealed jar or container until ready to serve.

This chutney will keep for up to 1 week in the refrigerator.

YIELD
about ½ cup

PREP TIME
10 minutes

TOTAL TIME
10 minutes

199

DRESSINGS & SAUCES

YIELD
about 1 cup

PREP TIME
5 minutes

TOTAL TIME
5 minutes

PRESERVED LEMON VINAIGRETTE

I've lived in several places with lemon trees and have always enjoyed preserving their surplus. This forced me to come up with creative uses for preserved lemons, one of which is this tart and tangy dressing.

1 whole preserved lemon (see p. 210)

¼ cup lemon juice

¼ cup apple cider vinegar

½ teaspoon honey (omit for vegan option*)

¼ cup olive oil

¼ teaspoon salt

In a blender, process together preserved lemon, water, vinegar and honey. Slowly drizzle in olive oil with the motor running. Add salt and blend a few seconds longer. Use immediately or transfer to a jar or sealed container and refrigerate.

This dressing will keep up to 10 days in the refrigerator.

* Honey is used here primarily as an emulsifying agent and less for sweetening (the preserved lemon's tartness and saltiness overrides it). If you want to make this recipe vegan, you can omit it. Just be sure to blend the dressing just prior to using it, as you will have a less stable emulsification without the honey.

DRESSINGS & SAUCES

PERSIMMON VINAIGRETTE

In the fall, when persimmons are bountiful, this is always my default salad dressing. Because persimmons are naturally high in pectin, this dressing should be made just before it is needed or else it will congeal. If this happens, you can restore its creaminess by running it through the blender again.

1 small Fuyu persimmon, cored and chopped

¼ cup white wine vinegar

½ cup grapeseed or other neutral oil

½ cup water

2 Tablespoons maple syrup

½-inch piece ginger, cut into coins

½ teaspoon salt

Place all ingredients except salt in a blender and puree. Add salt and process an additional few seconds. Taste and adjust any flavors to your liking. Use immediately.

YIELD
about 1¼ cup

PREP TIME
5 minutes

TOTAL TIME
5 minutes

DRESSINGS & SAUCES

YIELD
about 1½ cup

PREP TIME
5 minutes

TOTAL TIME
5 minutes

LEMON & HEMP SEED DRESSING

This tart and creamy dressing pairs especially well with bitter or pungent greens, like arugula and endive.

1 large lemon, peeled

½ cup hemp seeds

¾ cup coconut water

¼ cup apple cider vinegar

¼ cup olive oil

1 teaspoon salt

Place everything but the oil and salt in a blender and process until the lemon is pureed. Slowly drizzle in the oil while the motor runs. Add salt and process for a few seconds more. Use immediately or refrigerate in a tightly sealed jar or container.

This dressing will keep for up to 1 week in the refrigerator.

DRESSINGS & SAUCES

PARSLEY PECAN DRESSING

This dressing was inspired by one a friend made at a dinner I attended. Its slightly sour, very herbaceous flavor adds a spring-like touch to any salad.

½ cup raw pecans

¼ cup apple cider vinegar

1 bunch parsley, roughly chopped

¼ cup grapeseed or other neutral oil

½ teaspoon salt

Place pecans, vinegar and parsley in a blender. Process for about 30 seconds, or until nuts and parsley are chopped. Slowly drizzle in the oil and let blender run just until a creamy consistency is achieved. Add salt and process for a couple seconds more. Taste and adjust any flavors as desired. Add 1-2 tablespoons of water if you prefer a thinner dressing. Use immediately or refrigerate in a tightly sealed jar or container.

This dressing will keep for up to 1 week in the refrigerator.

YIELD
about 1 cup

PREP TIME
5 minutes

TOTAL TIME
5 minutes

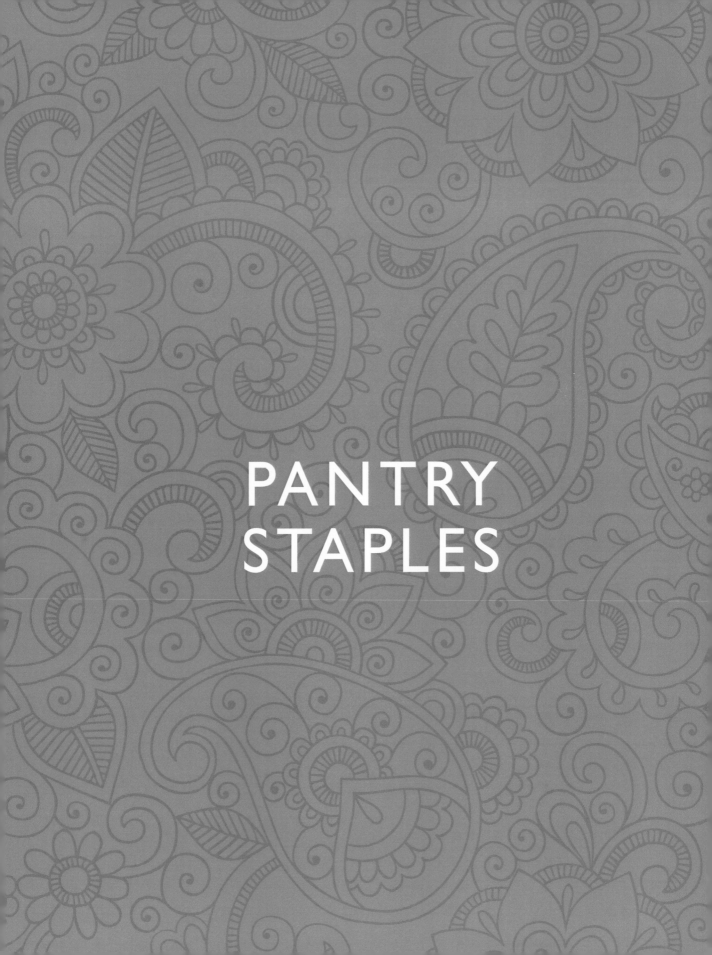

PANTRY STAPLES

VEGETABLE BROTH

GHEE

FLAX EGGS

ALMOND PARMESAN

PRESERVED LEMONS

ALMOND MILK

HEMP MILK

ZA'ATAR

GARAM MASALA

DIGESTIVE CHURNA

PANTRY STAPLES

YIELD
about 2½ quarts

PREP TIME
5 minutes

COOK TIME
1 hour

TOTAL TIME
1 hour +
5 minutes

VEGETABLE BROTH

Vegetable broth is the golden nectar of plant-based cooking. I encourage you to keep a large container or quart-sized bag in your freezer and put all viable vegetable scraps in it each time you cook. This could include things like stems and ends, skins, tough or bruised pieces, herb stalks, etc. Once the bag is full, you're ready to make a batch of broth (or you can make a smaller batch at any point). You can add additional ingredients to your scraps as well. I always like to include a couple mushrooms for umami flavor and some fresh parsley.

Approximately 1 quart of vegetable scraps

Place scraps in a large stockpot and add enough water to cover them by about an inch. Bring the pot to a boil over high heat, and then reduce heat, cover pot and simmer for 1 hour. Strain scraps out of broth and transfer broth to jars or containers.

Once broth is fully cooled, refrigerate or freeze it for later use. Broth will last up to 6 months in the freezer.

·· **BROTH TIPS** ··

Adding ginger to your broth will make it more pungent

·········

Include sweet potato or winter squash for a sweeter broth

·········

Broth will be a bit cloudier if you include potato skins or pieces

·········

Avoid using beets or purple potato skins in your broth unless you want a blueish hue

·········

Feel free to add peppercorns or other whole spices

·········

GHEE

YIELD
about 1 pint

PREP TIME
5 minutes

COOK TIME
40 minutes

TOTAL TIME
45 minutes
+ cooling

Ghee is an essential ingredient in Ayurvedic cooking and a wonderfully nutritive and tonifying food. Ghee is clarified butter, meaning all the milkfat is removed. There are many wonderful organic ghees available to purchase, but I prefer making my own. The traditional method is to make ghee on the stove, but this can be tricky (especially on electric ranges) because it can easily burn while cooking. Once I discovered this oven method, I was instantly hooked.

1 pound good quality butter (ideally organic and grass-fed)

Preheat oven to 250 degrees.

Place butter in a small Dutch oven or other oven-proof baking dish, then place in oven uncovered. Cook for 40 minutes, and then check ghee for readiness. To do this, dip a corner of a paper towel into the ghee and then try to light it with a match or lighter (keep a small glass of water nearby to extinguish the flame). If it burns like a candle, your ghee is done. If it does not, continue to cook ghee in the oven, checking every 5 minutes until you find it is done using the paper towel test.

When ghee has finished cooking, let is cool slightly. Carefully pour through cheesecloth* into one medium-sized jar or a few smaller jars. Remove cheesecloth and discard the milkfat solids that have collected. Let ghee cool completely; then cover and store. Ghee will solidify as it cools and does not need to be refrigerated.

I line a small sieve with cheesecloth and place it over the jar. You can also use rubber bands to tightly secure cheesecloth over the opening of a jar.

PANTRY STAPLES

REPLACES
1 egg

PREP TIME
5 minutes

CHILL TIME
20 minutes

TOTAL TIME
25 minutes

FLAX EGGS

Flax eggs are regarded as one of the best substitutes for the real thing in plant-based baking. The key to getting the best results is to chill the flax mixture before using, so always plan ahead to allow yourself enough time. I usually make these and then use the time while they are chilling to assemble all my other ingredients.

1 Tablespoon ground flaxseed meal*

2 Tablespoon filtered water

Whisk together flaxseed and water in a small bowl. Chill in refrigerator 15–20 minutes before using as an egg replacer in baking recipes.

* Pre-ground flaxseed is very volatile and can spoil easily, so always store it in the refrigerator in a dark or opaque container. You can grind you own meal in a high-powered blender. It can be hard to get a fine enough consistency when grinding just a tablespoon or two at a time, so I recommend doing at least a ½ cup and storing it as recommended.

PANTRY STAPLES

ALMOND PARMESAN

YIELD
about ⅓ cup

PREP TIME
5 minutes

TOTAL TIME
5 minutes

This is almost always in my refrigerator and is my favorite topping for the many pasta dishes my husband loves to make. It can also be tossed with sautéed greens or mixed into kale salads for a nutty texture and flavor.

¼ cup raw almonds

2 Tablespoons nutritional yeast

1 large clove garlic, cut into quarters

⅛ teaspoon salt

Place almonds in a mini food processor (a standard food processor or blender can be used as well) and process until roughly chopped. Add remaining ingredients and run machine until everything is uniformly processed and roughly resembles the texture of parmesan cheese.

Store almond parmesan in a tightly-sealed jar or container in the refrigerator, where it will keep for up to 2 months.

PANTRY STAPLES

YIELD
8–10 lemons

PREP TIME
15 minutes

TOTAL TIME
15 minutes
+ resting

PRESERVED LEMONS

When life gives people lemons, some like to make lemonade, but I personally choose to preserve them. Preserved lemons are an essential ingredient in Moroccan cooking, and a jar of them always makes a wonderful gift for foodie friends that love to cook. You can add any number of flavor elements to your lemons (see opposite page), but I personally lean towards a minimalist approach.

8–10 small lemons, washed

¾ cup Kosher or other coarse salt

Additional fresh-squeezed lemon juice

Olive oil

Cut a deep "X" into each lemon, starting at the top (stem) end and stopping about ¼ inch from the bottom.

Use your fingers to gently open each lemon, working over a shallow bowl or pie dish to catch any juices that may run out. Stuff each lemon with a few big pinches of salt, and then place into a clean quart-sized jar. Repeat the process with each lemon, using a tamper or the handle of a large wooden spoon to pack the lemons in.

After all lemons have been stuffed and packed, pour any excess juice/salt from your bowl into the jar. Add additional lemon juice as needed to cover the lemons in the jar, and seal it well. Let the jar sit in a cool, dark place for 1 month. Lemons are then ready to use.

Once I begin using a jar of lemons, I like to pour a thin layer of olive oil into the top of the jar to help inhibit white mold growth. If mold does appear, it is harmless and can be rinsed off your lemons. Make sure that each time you use a lemon, all remaining lemons stay submerged under the juice/oil. Preserved lemons will keep for up to 6 months.

When you are ready to use a preserved lemon, scrape out the flesh and seeds and rinse the rind under cool water to remove excess salt unless a recipe directs otherwise.

PANTRY STAPLES

·· OPTIONAL FLAVOR ELEMENTS ··

bay leaves

· · · · · · · ·

cinnamon sticks

· · · · · · · ·

coriander seeds

· · · · · · · ·

cumin seeds

· · · · · · · ·

dried red chiles

· · · · · · · ·

fennel seeds

· · · · · · · ·

peppercorns

· · · · · · · ·

rosemary sprigs

· · · · · · · ·

PANTRY STAPLES

YIELD
about 1 quart

PREP TIME
5 minutes

TOTAL TIME
5 minutes

HEMP MILK

I love the nutty, complex flavor of hemp milk and find it's a great non-dairy complement for tea and coffee. Hemp is one of the best plant-based sources of omega fatty acids, making it a nutritionally sound pick as well.

1 cup hemp seeds

3½ cups filtered water

Pinch of salt

Place hemp seeds and water in a blender and process on a high speed for 1 minute. Transfer hemp milk to a large jar or container and refrigerate. You can optionally strain hemp milk through a nut milk bag, although I usually skip this to retain the full nutrition of the hemp seeds.

Hemp milk will last 4–5 days maximum in the refrigerator. Your nose will tell you when it is no longer good. Hemp milk will separate while stored, so always give it a good shake before using.

PANTRY STAPLES

ALMOND MILK

YIELD
about 1 quart

PREP TIME
5 minutes

TOTAL TIME
5 minutes

Fresh almond milk is divine, and once you start making your own, you won't want to drink any from a box. The key to making silky smooth milk is to purchase a nut milk bag. These are easily found online or in some kitchen stores or health food markets.

1 cup raw almonds, soaked minimum 4 hours and drained

4 cups water

Place almonds and water in a blender and process on high speed for 1 minute. Pour almond milk through a nut milk bag into a large pitcher or container below. Use one hand to hold the bag shut and the other to squeeze the bag until no liquid escapes and pulp is on the drier side. Leftover pulp can be used for baking or added to smoothies. Transfer the milk to a large jar or other sealed container.

Almond milk will keep 4–5 days maximum in the refrigerator. Your nose will tell you when it is no longer good. Almond milk will separate while stored, so always give it a good shake before using.

· · CUSTOMIZATIONS · ·

Add 1–2 dates for sweetness or vanilla bean powder/vanilla extract for flavor

· · · · · · · ·

Raw cacao can be added (along with dates or maple syrup) for a chocolate version

· · · · · · · ·

Fresh mango or strawberry can lend a fruity feel

· · · · · · · ·

ZA'ATAR

YIELD
1 small jar

PREP TIME
5 minutes

COOK TIME
5 minutes

TOTAL TIME
10 minutes

Some of my favorite memories of traveling in the Middle East involve meals that began with a simple appetizer of pita bread with olive oil and za'atar. This spice mix from the region has infinite variations, but pretty much always contains ground sumac (a slightly tart berry) and sesame seeds. My version is a bit untraditional because it includes mint, but I absolutely love the flavor it lends.

- 2 Tablespoons sesame seeds
- 1 Tablespoon sumac
- 1 teaspoon dried oregano
- 1 teaspoon dried thyme
- ¼ teaspoon dried mint
- ½ teaspoon salt

Heat a small skillet over medium heat. Add sesame seeds and toast for 1-2 minutes, or until fragrant and very lightly browned. Transfer seeds to a small jar.

Once sesame seeds are cool, add all remaining ingredients to the jar and shake well.

PANTRY STAPLES

YIELD
1 small jar

PREP TIME
5 minutes

TOTAL TIME
5 minutes

GARAM MASALA

Garam masala is a generic term for any blend of pungent spices in Indian cooking. This is my personal favorite mix, although countless recipes exist.

½ teaspoon ground cinnamon

½ teaspoon ground clove

½ teaspoon ground cumin

½ teaspoon ground coriander

¼ teaspoon ground ginger

¼ teaspoon ground cardamom

Place all ingredients in a small jar and shake well.

PANTRY STAPLES

DIGESTIVE CHURNA

YIELD
1 small jar

PREP TIME
5 minutes

TOTAL TIME
5 minutes

Churnas are spice mixes used in Ayurveda to facilitate digestion and to help alleviate other conditions. This basic blend helps fuel our digestive fire and adds flavor to otherwise plain foods like steamed or roasted vegetables, grains, etc. I enjoy sprinkling it on fresh fruit as well.

2 teaspoons fennel seeds

2 teaspoons coriander seeds

1 teaspoon cumin seeds

1 teaspoon ground ginger

1 teaspoon turmeric powder

Blend all ingredients using a coffee grinder, spice mill, or mortar and pestle until a uniform powder is achieved. Store in a jar or other sealed container. Sprinkle a few pinches on anything you wish.

GRATITUDE & ACKNOWLEDGEMENTS

This book would not be possible without the encouragement of all the many people who have sat at my table during the decade of my life that I have spent cooking professionally. To everyone who has dined on my food at retreats and parties and via weekly meal delivery, thank you for your support and allowing me to nourish you.

I am grateful to all my teachers who have guided me on life's path, most notably *Edward Espe Brown*, who taught me to lighten up and enjoy myself in the kitchen, and *Thich Nhat Hanh*, who made me appreciate dishwashing in ways I never knew I could. And to my first cooking teacher, *Judy Greenberg,* aka mi madre, thank you for letting me get my hands dirty in the kitchen from a very young age.

I am delighted that *Amy Saidens* supported this project with her brilliant design talents. Thank you, Amy, for bringing my visions to reality and dedicating so much time to this book. I couldn't be more thrilled with the way it looks.

Thank you to *Tessa & Sammy* of Blooming Bites Photography for the wonderful photos that grace the pages of this book and for making each shoot so fun and relaxed.

Thank you to *Mallory Greene* for the stellar editing support and to *Wendy Allex* for the careful indexing work that allows readers to navigate this book with ease.

I am grateful I stumbled upon the amazingly talented *Nicole Pilar* at a festival years ago and that she was enthusiastic about sending a box of her beautiful dishware cross-country so I could feature it here. All of the organic oyster shell dishware you see here was crafted by her hands in Brooklyn.

Additional gratitude goes to the following people who have supported me and my creative endeavors in the kitchen over the years, both as clients and as friends, as well as the people who assisted the creation of this book through recipe testing, sharing book publishing experiences, and so much more: *Chrisandra Fox-Walker, Chaz Russ, Karen Macklin, Daniel Stewart, Lisa Scheff, Christine Mason-Miller, Shawnna Stewart and Erik Olson, Carrie Lederer and Matt Hollingsworth, Jacqueline Kim, Elaine Klein, Liz Kalloch, Megan Cauley, Heather Law,* and *Jessica Kelsh.*

Thank you to my husband, *Francis DellaVecchia*, for being my biggest fan and lifelong taste tester (and always eating all the leftovers).

Most of all, thank you, dear readers, for bringing the recipes of this book to life.

INDEX

A

Almonds:
    Almond Milk, 213
    Almond Parmesan, 209
    Miso Soup with Vegetables & Almonds, 66–67
    Quinoa with Currants and Almonds, 102
    Romesco Sauce, 193
Appetizers & snacks:
    Arugula & Artichoke Dip, 45
    Black Lentil Hummus, 42
    Classic Hummus, 40
    Cooling Cucumber Guacamole, 49
    Curried Red Lentil Dip, 44
    Garam Masala Popcorn, 50
    Guacamole Three Ways, 48–49
    Mango Jalapeño Guacamole, 49
    Marinated Mushrooms with Garlic Macadamia "Cheese," 38–39
    Roasted Butternut Squash Hummus, 41
    Zesty Kale Chips, 46–47
Apples:
    Butternut Squash, Fuji Apple & Chipotle Soup, 56
    Fall Harvest Salad, 128
Artichoke Dip, Arugula &, 45
Arugula & Artichoke Dip, 45
Arugula & Radish Salad, 129
Asparagus, Watercress & Cauliflower Soup, 70–71
Autumn Vegetable Tagine, 90–91
Avocados:
    Chilled Cucumber & Avocado Soup, 55
    Chocolate Avocado Pudding, 164
    Corn, Tomato & Avocado Salad, 125
    Guacamole Three Ways, 48–49

B

Baked Zucchini Boats, 92–93
Bananas:
    Banana Bread, 26–27
    Banana Buckwheat Pancakes, 29
    Date Shake, 187
    Hemp Protein Smoothie, 187
    Tropical Green Smoothie, 186
Basic Beans, 110
Basil Dandelion Pesto, 192
Basmati Rice Pilau, 106
Beans:
    Basic Beans, 110
    Beetloaf, 82
    Black Bean & Edamame Salad, 118
    Classic Hummus, 40
    Green Chile Stew, 111
    Kitchari, 83
    Mung Dal Tadka, 114
    Potato & Green Bean Subji, 156
    Roasted Butternut Squash Hummus, 41
    White Bean Ragout with Sundried Tomatoes, 113
Beet, Kale & Pomegranate Salad, 122
Beetloaf, 82
Black Bean & Edamame Salad, 118
Black Lentil Hummus, 42
Black Rice and Roasted Pineapple Salad, 100
Blood Orange & Thyme Sorbet, 172
Breakfast:
    Banana Bread, 26–27
    Banana Buckwheat Pancakes, 29
    Chia Seed Pudding Breakfast Bowls, 32
    Coconut Pecan Scones, 34–35
    Curried Steel-Cut Oats, 25
    Quinoa Porridge, 30
    Savory Millet Cereal, 20
    Spiced Maple Pecan Granola, 22–23
    Steel-Cut Oats with Persimmon, Dates & Toasted Pumpkin Seeds, 24
    Tofu Garden Scramble, 31
Broccoli with Meyer Lemon, Roasted, 150
Brussels Sprouts, Maple-Balsamic, 146
Buckwheat Pancakes, Banana, 29
Butternut Squash, Fuji Apple & Chipotle Soup, 56
Butternut Squash & Sage Risotto, 86–87

C

Cabbage & Shiitakes, Stir-Fried Savoy, 151
Capers, Roasted Cauliflower with, 139
Carrots:
    Carrot, Daikon & Hijiki Stir-Fry, 153
    Sweet Za'atar Carrots, 137
Cashews:
    Cashew Crème, 174–175
    Chipotle Cashew Cream, 197
    Raw Piña Colada "Cheese" Cake, 170–171
    Zesty Kale Chips, 46–47
Cauliflower:
    Asparagus, Watercress & Cauliflower Soup, 70–71
    Grilled Cauliflower Steaks with Harissa, 88
    Moroccan Cauliflower, 157
    Roasted Cauliflower with Capers, 139
Charmoula, 195
Chia Seed Pudding Breakfast Bowls, 32
Chiles. See Peppers
Chilled Cucumber & Avocado Soup, 55
Chimichurri, 194
Chipotle Cashew Cream, 197

INDEX

Chipotle Salsa, Tomatillo, 190
Chipotle Soup, Butternut Squash, Fuji Apple &, 56
Chocolate Avocado Pudding, 164
Cilantro:
    Charmoula, 195
    Chimichurri, 194
    Cilantro Coconut Chutney, 199
    Roasted Eggplant with Cilantro, 154
Cilantro Coconut Chutney, 199
Classic Hummus, 40
Coconut Chutney, Cilantro, 199
Coconut Curry Dal, 117
Coconut Curry Lentil Soup, 58
Coconut Fennel Chowder, 54
Coconut Pecan Scones, 34–35
Collard Wraps with Shiitake-Sunflower Seed Pâté, 78–79
Cooling Cucumber Guacamole, 49
Coriander, Fennel & Cumin Tea, 181
Corn, Tomato & Avocado Salad, 125
Creamy Dijon Tempeh, 94
Cucumbers:
    Chilled Cucumber & Avocado Soup, 55
    Cooling Cucumber Guacamole, 49
    Cucumber Yogurt Mint Soup, 65
    Quinoa Tabbouleh, 103
    Springtime Salad with Kumquats, 126
Cumin:
    Coriander, Fennel & Cumin Tea, 181
    Garam Masala, 216
    Lebanese Lentil Soup, 59
Currants and Almonds, Quinoa with, 102
Curry powder:
    Coconut Curry Dal, 117
    Coconut Curry Lentil Soup, 58
    Curried Red Lentil Dip, 44
    Curried Steel-Cut Oats, 25

D Daikon & Hijiki Stir-Fry, Carrot, 153
Dandelion Pesto, Basil, 192
Dates:
    Chocolate Avocado Pudding, 164
    Date Shake, 187
    Golden Rose Milk, 182
    Moroccan Date Cake, 162–163
    Most Perfect Date, The, 167
    Perfect Date, The, 165
    Raw Piña Colada "Cheese" Cake, 170–171
    Steel-Cut Oats with Persimmon,
        Dates & Toasted Pumpkin Seeds, 24

Dessert:
    Blood Orange & Thyme Sorbet, 172
    Cashew Crème, 174–175
    Chocolate Avocado Pudding, 164
    Easy Peach Cobbler, 169
    Moroccan Date Cake, 162–163
    Most Perfect Date, The, 167
    Orange Poppy Seed Pudding, 168
    Perfect Date, The, 165
    Raw Piña Colada "Cheese" Cake, 170–171
Dijon Dill Potatoes, 158
Dressings:
    Lemon & Hemp Seed Dressing, 202
    Parsley Pecan Dressing, 203
    Persimmon Vinaigrette, 201
    Preserved Lemon Vinaigrette, 200
    Tahini Garlic Dressing, 197

E Easy Peach Cobbler, 169
Edamame Salad, Black Bean &, 118
Eggplant:
    Roasted Eggplant with Cilantro, 154
    Toasted Farro Salad with Roasted Vegetables, 105

F Fall Harvest Salad, 128
Farro Salad with Roasted Vegetables, Toasted, 105
Fennel:
    Coconut Fennel Chowder, 54
    Coriander, Fennel & Cumin Tea, 181
    Orange, Olive & Fennel Salad, 130
Flax Eggs, 208
French Green Lentil Salad, 119

G Garam Masala, 216
Garam Masala Popcorn, 50
Garlic:
    Marinated Mushrooms with Garlic Macadamia "Cheese," 38–39
    Rosemary Garlic Polenta, 98
    Tahini Garlic Dressing, 197
Gazpacho, Rustic Watermelon, 68
Ghee, 207
Ginger:
    Mango Ginger Chutney, 199
    Maple-Ginger Glazed Acorn Squash, 143
    Pranaful Chai, 179
Golden Rose Milk, 182
Grains:
    Basmati Rice Pilau, 106
    Black Rice and Roasted Pineapple Salad, 100

INDEX

Millet with Sweet Potato & Olives, 99
Quinoa Tabbouleh, 103
Quinoa with Currants and Almonds, 102
Rosemary Garlic Polenta, 98
Toasted Farro Salad with Roasted Vegetables, 105
Green Chile Stew, 111
Gremolata, 195
Grilled Cauliflower Steaks with Harissa, 88
Guacamole Three Ways, 48-49

H
Harissa, 196
Harissa, Grilled Cauliflower Steaks with, 88
Hazelnuts:
    Baked Zucchini Boats, 92-93
    Romesco Sauce, 193
    Zucchini with Hazelnut Crumble, 138
Heartwarmer Tea, 181
Hemp Milk, 212
Hemp Protein Smoothie, 187
Hemp Seed Dressing, Lemon &, 202
Hijiki Stir-Fry, Carrot, Daikon &, 153
Horseradish Mashed Potatoes, 147
Hummus:
    Black Lentil Hummus, 42
    Classic Hummus, 40
    Roasted Butternut Squash Hummus, 41

J
Jackfruit Fesenjan, 80-81
Jalapeño Guacamole, Mango, 49

K
Kale:
    Beet, Kale & Pomegranate Salad, 122
    Hemp Protein Smoothie, 187
    Simple Greens, 142
    Tahini Kale Salad, 132
    Tropical Green Smoothie, 186
    Winter Kale Salad, 123
    Zesty Kale Chips, 46-47
Kitchari, 83
Kumquats, Springtime Salad with, 126

L
Lebanese Lentil Soup, 59
Leek Soup, Smoky Potato, 60
Legumes:
    Basic Beans, 110
    Black Bean & Edamame Salad, 118
    Coconut Curry Dal, 117
    French Green Lentil Salad, 119
    Green Chile Stew, 111

Mung Dal Tadka, 114
Red Lentil Dal with Tamarind, 116
White Bean Ragout with Sundried Tomatoes, 113
Lemons:
    Lemon & Hemp Seed Dressing, 202
    Moroccan Cauliflower, 157
    Preserved Lemons, 210-211
    Preserved Lemon Vinaigrette, 200
    Roasted Broccoli with Meyer Lemon, 150
Lemon Verbena & Mint Tea, 184
Lentils:
    Black Lentil Hummus, 42
    Coconut Curry Dal, 117
    Coconut Curry Lentil Soup, 58
    Curried Red Lentil Dip, 44
    French Green Lentil Salad, 119
    Lebanese Lentil Soup, 59
    Lentil Shepherd's Pie, 76-77
    Moroccan Harira, 63
    Red Lentil Dal with Tamarind, 116
Lettuce:
    Raw Tacos, 74
    Springtime Salad with Kumquats, 126

M
Macadamia "Cheese," Marinated Mushrooms with Garlic, 38-39
Mains:
    Autumn Vegetable Tagine, 90-91
    Baked Zucchini Boats, 92-93
    Beetloaf, 82
    Butternut Squash & Sage Risotto, 86-87
    Collard Wraps with Shiitake-Sunflower Seed Pâté, 78-79
    Creamy Dijon Tempeh, 94
    Grilled Cauliflower Steaks with Harissa, 88
    Jackfruit Fesenjan, 80-81
    Kitchari, 83
    Lentil Shepherd's Pie, 76-77
    Raw Tacos, 74
    Zucchini Walnut Pasta, 85
Mango Ginger Chutney, 199
Mango Jalapeño Guacamole, 49
Millet:
    Millet with Sweet Potato & Olives, 99
    Savory Millet Cereal, 20
Mint:
    Cucumber Yogurt Mint Soup, 65
    Lebanese Lentil Soup, 59
    Lemon Verbena & Mint Tea, 184
    Moroccan Mint Tea, 180
Miso Soup with Vegetables & Almonds, 66-67

INDEX

Moroccan Acorn Squash & Pear Soup, 62
Moroccan Cauliflower, 157
Moroccan Date Cake, 162–163
Moroccan Harira, 63
Moroccan Mint Tea, 180
Most Perfect Date, The, 167
Mung Dal Tadka, 114
Mushrooms:
    Collard Wraps with Shiitake-Sunflower Seed Pâté, 78–79
    Lentil Shepherd's Pie, 76–77
    Marinated Mushrooms with Garlic Macadamia "Cheese," 38–39
    Sautéed Mixed Mushrooms, 140
    Stir-Fried Savoy Cabbage & Shiitakes, 151
    Tofu Garden Scramble, 31
Mustard, Dijon:
    Creamy Dijon Tempeh, 94
    Dijon Dill Potatoes, 158

O

Oats:
    Curried Steel-Cut Oats, 25
    Easy Peach Cobbler, 169
    Spiced Maple Pecan Granola, 22–23
    Steel-Cut Oats with Persimmon, Dates & Toasted Pumpkin Seeds, 24
Okra with Peanuts, Spiced, 148
Olives:
    Millet with Sweet Potato & Olives, 99
    Orange, Olive & Fennel Salad, 130
Oranges:
    Blood Orange & Thyme Sorbet, 172
    Heartwarmer Tea, 181
    Orange, Olive & Fennel Salad, 130
    Orange Poppy Seed Pudding, 168

P

Parsley:
    Charmoula, 195
    Chimichurri, 194
    Gremolata, 195
    Parsley Pecan Dressing, 203
Pasta:
    Moroccan Harira, 63
    Zucchini Walnut Pasta, 85
Peach Cobbler, Easy, 169
Peanuts, Spiced Okra with, 148
Pears:
    Fall Harvest Salad, 128
    Moroccan Acorn Squash & Pear Soup, 62
    Winter Kale Salad, 123
Peas:
    Green Chile Stew, 111
    Springtime Salad with Kumquats, 126
Pecans:
    Coconut Pecan Scones, 34–35
    Parsley Pecan Dressing, 203
    Spiced Maple Pecan Granola, 22–23
Peppers:
    Butternut Squash, Fuji Apple & Chipotle Soup, 56
    Chipotle Cashew Cream, 197
    Green Chile Stew, 111
    Harissa, 196
    Mango Jalapeño Guacamole, 49
    Romesco Sauce, 193
    Tofu Garden Scramble, 31
    Tomatillo Chipotle Salsa, 190
Perfect Date, The, 165
Persimmon:
    Fall Harvest Salad, 128
    Persimmon Vinaigrette, 201
    Steel-Cut Oats with Persimmon, Dates & Toasted Pumpkin Seeds, 24
Pesto, Basil Dandelion, 192
Piña Colada "Cheese" Cake, Raw, 170–171
Pineapple:
    Black Rice and Roasted Pineapple Salad, 100
    Raw Piña Colada "Cheese" Cake, 170–171
    Tropical Green Smoothie, 186
Polenta, Rosemary Garlic, 98
Pomegranate Salad, Beet, Kale &, 122
Popcorn, Garam Masala, 50
Poppy Seed Pudding, Orange, 168
Potatoes:
    Dijon Dill Potatoes, 158
    Horseradish Mashed Potatoes, 147
    Potato & Green Bean Subji, 156
    Smoky Potato Leek Soup, 60
    See also Sweet potatoes
Pranaful Chai, 179
Preserved Lemons, 210–211
Preserved Lemon Vinaigrette, 200
Pumpkin seeds:
    Basil Dandelion Pesto, 192
    Steel-Cut Oats with Persimmon, Dates & Toasted Pumpkin Seeds, 24

Q

Quinoa:
    Baked Zucchini Boats, 92–93
    Quinoa Porridge, 30
    Quinoa Tabbouleh, 103

INDEX

Quinoa with Currants and Almonds, 102

R
Radishes:
    Arugula & Radish Salad, 129
    Carrot, Daikon & Hijiki Stir-Fry, 153
Raw Piña Colada "Cheese" Cake, 170–171
Raw Tacos, 74
Red Lentil Dal with Tamarind, 116
Rice:
    Basmati Rice Pilau, 106
    Black Rice and Roasted Pineapple Salad, 100
    Butternut Squash & Sage Risotto, 86–87
    Kitchari, 83
Roasted Broccoli with Meyer Lemon, 150
Roasted Butternut Squash Hummus, 41
Roasted Cauliflower with Capers, 139
Roasted Eggplant with Cilantro, 154
Romesco Sauce, 193
Rosemary Garlic Polenta, 98
Rustic Watermelon Gazpacho, 68

S
Sage Risotto, Butternut Squash &, 86–87
Salads:
    Arugula & Radish Salad, 129
    Beet, Kale & Pomegranate Salad, 122
    Black Bean & Edamame Salad, 118
    Corn, Tomato & Avocado Salad, 125
    Fall Harvest Salad, 128
    French Green Lentil Salad, 119
    Orange, Olive & Fennel Salad, 130
    Springtime Salad with Kumquats, 126
    Tahini Kale Salad, 132
    Winter Kale Salad, 123
Sauces:
    Basil Dandelion Pesto, 192
    Charmoula, 195
    Chimichurri, 194
    Chipotle Cashew Cream, 197
    Cilantro Coconut Chutney, 199
    Gremolata, 195
    Harissa, 196
    Mango Ginger Chutney, 199
    Romesco Sauce, 193
    Tomatillo Chipotle Salsa, 190
Sautéed Mixed Mushrooms, 140
Savory Millet Cereal, 20
Seeds:
    Basil Dandelion Pesto, 192
    Chia Seed Pudding Breakfast Bowls, 32
    Collard Wraps with Shiitake-Sunflower Seed Pâté, 78–79
    Lemon & Hemp Seed Dressing, 202
    Orange Poppy Seed Pudding, 168
    Steel-Cut Oats with Persimmon, Dates & Toasted Pumpkin Seeds, 24
    Za'atar, 215
Simple Greens, 142
Smoky Potato Leek Soup, 60
Smoothies:
    Date Shake, 187
    Hemp Protein Smoothie, 187
    Tropical Green Smoothie, 186
Snacks. See Appetizers & snacks
Soups:
    Asparagus, Watercress & Cauliflower Soup, 70–71
    Butternut Squash, Fuji Apple & Chipotle Soup, 56
    Chilled Cucumber & Avocado Soup, 55
    Coconut Curry Lentil Soup, 58
    Coconut Fennel Chowder, 54
    Cucumber Yogurt Mint Soup, 65
    Lebanese Lentil Soup, 59
    Miso Soup with Vegetables & Almonds, 66–67
    Moroccan Acorn Squash & Pear Soup, 62
    Moroccan Harira, 63
    Rustic Watermelon Gazpacho, 68
    Smoky Potato Leek Soup, 60
Spiced Maple Pecan Granola, 22–23
Spiced Okra with Peanuts, 148
Springtime Salad with Kumquats, 126
Squash:
    Butternut Squash, Fuji Apple & Chipotle Soup, 56
    Butternut Squash & Sage Risotto, 86–87
    Maple-Ginger Glazed Acorn Squash, 143
    Moroccan Acorn Squash & Pear Soup, 62
    Roasted Butternut Squash Hummus, 41
    Toasted Farro Salad with Roasted Vegetables, 105
Staples, pantry:
    Almond Milk, 213
    Almond Parmesan, 209
    Flax Eggs, 208
    Garam Masala, 216
    Ghee, 207
    Hemp Milk, 212
    Preserved Lemons, 210–211
    Vegetable Broth, 206
    Za'atar, 215
Steel-Cut Oats with Persimmon, Dates & Toasted Pumpkin Seeds, 24
Stir-Fried Savoy Cabbage & Shiitakes, 151

INDEX

Sunflower Seed Pâté, Collard Wraps with Shiitake-, 78–79
Sweet potatoes:
    Lentil Shepherd's Pie, 76–77
    Millet with Sweet Potato & Olives, 99
    Miso Soup with Vegetables & Almonds, 66–67
    Turmeric Sweet Potato Hash, 145
    See also Potatoes
Sweet Za'atar Carrots, 137

T

Tacos, Raw, 74
Tahini:
    Black Lentil Hummus, 42
    Classic Hummus, 40
    Tahini Garlic Dressing, 197
    Tahini Kale Salad, 132
Tamarind, Red Lentil Dal with, 116
Teas:
    Coriander, Fennel & Cumin Tea, 181
    Golden Rose Milk, 182
    Heartwarmer Tea, 181
    Lemon Verbena & Mint Tea, 184
    Matcha Latte, 185
    Moroccan Mint Tea, 180
    Pranaful Chai, 179
Tempeh, Creamy Dijon, 94
Thyme Sorbet, Blood Orange &, 172
Toasted Farro Salad with Roasted Vegetables, 105
Tofu Garden Scramble, 31
Tomatillo Chipotle Salsa, 190
Tomatoes:
    Corn, Tomato & Avocado Salad, 125
    Harissa, 196
    Moroccan Harira, 63
    Mung Dal Tadka, 114
    Quinoa Tabbouleh, 103
    Raw Tacos, 74
    Romesco Sauce, 193
    Rustic Watermelon Gazpacho, 68
    White Bean Ragout with Sundried Tomatoes, 113
Tropical Green Smoothie, 186
Turmeric Sweet Potato Hash, 145

V

Vegetable Broth, 206
Vegetable Tagine, Autumn, 90–91
Veggie sides:
    Carrot, Daikon & Hijiki Stir-Fry, 153
    Dijon Dill Potatoes, 158
    Horseradish Mashed Potatoes, 147
    Maple-Balsamic Brussels Sprouts, 146
    Maple-Ginger Glazed Acorn Squash, 143
    Moroccan Cauliflower, 157
    Potato & Green Bean Subji, 156
    Roasted Broccoli with Meyer Lemon, 150
    Roasted Cauliflower with Capers, 139
    Roasted Eggplant with Cilantro, 154
    Sautéed Mixed Mushrooms, 140
    Simple Greens, 142
    Spiced Okra with Peanuts, 148
    Stir-Fried Savoy Cabbage & Shiitakes, 151
    Sweet Za'atar Carrots, 137
    Turmeric Sweet Potato Hash, 145
    Zucchini with Hazelnut Crumble, 138
Vinegar:
    Maple-Balsamic Brussels Sprouts, 146
    Persimmon Vinaigrette, 201
    Preserved Lemon Vinaigrette, 200

W

Walnuts:
    Basil Dandelion Pesto, 192
    Jackfruit Fesenjan, 80–81
    Most Perfect Date, The, 167
    Raw Tacos, 74
    Zucchini Walnut Pasta, 85
Watercress & Cauliflower Soup, Asparagus, 70–71
Watermelon Gazpacho, Rustic, 68
White Bean Ragout with Sundried Tomatoes, 113
Winter Kale Salad, 123

Y

Yogurt Mint Soup, Cucumber, 65

Z

Za'atar, 215
Za'atar Carrots, Sweet, 137
Zesty Kale Chips, 46–47
Zucchini:
    Baked Zucchini Boats, 92–93
    Toasted Farro Salad with Roasted Vegetables, 105
    Zucchini Walnut Pasta, 85
    Zucchini with Hazelnut Crumble, 138

KITCHEN RITUAL TEAM

MEREDITH KLEIN
Author

Meredith Klein is a Los Angeles-based chef who is passionate about helping individuals experience radical transformation through the practices of meditation and healthy, mindful eating. Meredith creates internationally inspired, Ayurvedically influenced organic cuisine and offers retreats, cooking classes, and individual consultations to support others in their journeys to eat well. A student of Zen Master Thich Nhat Hanh, Meredith also teaches meditation at retreats and workshops, in addition to offering one-on-one mindfulness-based life coaching.
Follow Meredith online at http://pranaful.com or search for Pranaful on social media platforms.

AMY SAIDENS
Designer

Amy Saidens is an artist and designer who looks and lives in Brooklyn, NY.
Follow her visual adventures on Instagram: @moreplumcakeplease.

TESSA DUFF AND SAMMY MILLER
Photographers

Tessa Duff and Sammy Miller are partners and co-founders of Blooming Bites Photography based in Culver City, CA. Both Tessa and Sammy were trained at Brooks Institute of Photography. They provide irresistible food photography and detailed food styling, all with ease and excitement.
http://bloomingbitesphotography.com

NICOLE PILAR
Tableware Artist

Brooklyn-based artist Nicole Pilar grew up just north of the city in a log cabin. The proximity to nature greatly influenced her artistic development. As an artist, Nicole explores mediums bringing out their most natural quality in the organic forms as reflected in her jewelry, home and tabletop collections, and installations. All of the handmade dishes seen in this book are her creations.
Learn more and shop at http://npilar.com